IDEOLOGY AND
MORAL PHILOSOPHY

IDEOLOGY AND MORAL PHILOSOPHY

The Relation of Moral Ideology
To Dynamic Moral Philosophy

by

K. BRUCE MILLER

HUMANITIES PRESS

New York   1971

To

J. LEVERING EVANS

Who First Inspired My Quest
Toward A Moral Ideology

ACKNOWLEDGMENTS

The Age of Ideology by Henry D. Aiken. Curtis Brown, Ltd. Copyright © 1956 by Henry D. Aiken. Reprinted by permission of the publisher.

The Origin of Russian Communism by Nicolas Berdyaev. Geoffrey Bles, Ltd., London. Copyright 1937. Reprinted through permission of the publisher. U.S.A. edition published by The University of Michigan Press, Ann Arbor. Copyright 1960. Reprinted through permission of the publisher.

From *The Two Sources of Morality and Religion* by Henri Bergson. Translated by R. Ashley Audra and Cloudesley Brereton with the assistance of W. Horsfall Carter. Copyright 1935, © 1963 by Holt, Rinehart and Winston, Inc. Reprinted by permission of Holt, Rinehart and Winston, Inc.

Soviet Scholasticism by Thomas J. Blakeley. D. Reidel Publishing Co., Dordrecht. Copyright 1961. Reprinted through permission of the publisher.

The Moral Nature of Man by A. Campbell Garnett. The Ronald Press Co., New York. Copyright © 1952. Reprinted through permission of the publisher.

"Vision and Choice in Morality," by R. W. Hepburn. Copyright 1956 by The Aristotelian Society. Reprinted by permission of The Aristotelian Society.

Contemporary Ethical Theories by T. E. Hill. The Macmillan Co. Copyright 1950. Reprinted through permission of the publisher.

Living Religions and a World Faith by William E. Hocking. George Allen & Unwin, Ltd. Copyright 1940. Reprinted through permission of the publisher.

Types of Philosophy by William E. Hocking. Charles Scribner's Sons. Copyright 1959. Reprinted through permission of the publisher.

"The Seriousness of Moral Philosophy" by Albert Hofstadter. *Ethics* LXVI (July, 1956). Copyright 1956. The University of Chicago Press. Reprinted through permission of the publisher.

Critique of Practical Reason: and Other Writings in Moral Philosophy by I. Kant. Translated and edited by L. W. Beck. The Bobbs-Merrill Company, Inc. Reprinted through permission of the publisher.

Relativism, Knowledge and Faith by Gordon Kaufman. The University of Chicago Press. Copyright 1960. Reprinted through permission of the author and publisher.

TABLE OF CONTENTS

PREFACE

The prime concern of this inquiry is the conceptual analysis, as a foundation to further synthesis, of dynamic morality. The subtitle of this inquiry suggests my basic presuppositions: I agree with Bergson that moral philosophy ought to be dynamic; this *dynamic* depends upon a relatedness or relational approach in moral philosophy; this relational approach of knowing, believing (including valuing), and doing constitutes the philosophical schema of an ideology (Ap. 1—7).

Prior to my awareness of the nature of ideology, I found my very being totally and suddenly captured in August, 1945, by the shocking realization that I was a citizen of an atomic age which immediately called for a far deeper commitment on my part to the deepest needs of humanity. Prior to this date, my consuming professional interest as a high school student had been in physics (i.e. in things); but from then onward I was convinced that I could only be true to myself and God's order in the world on the basis of a firm commitment to ultimate ends which were capable of controlling the instrumental colossus of atomic energy. This would require my commitment to something with an amount of moral *dynamic* at least equal to the problems raised by the implications of nuclear physics, including the survival of our basic values.

This dynamic morality was obvious to me in the living and thinking of the Hebrew prophets, the Apostles, and later men like St. Patrick, St. Francis, Luther, Wesley, Finney, and Buchman; however, the strange phenomenon which has emerged in this generation is that *dynamic* has generally appeared in the greatest quantity in the evil ideologies of Fascism, Nazism, and Marxism-Leninism. This struck me profoundly during World War II and the post-war period where the leaders of the free world seemed to be stymied by the ideological machinations of the Marxist-Leninists who could even manipulate the good will of the West toward self-destruction. They had a clear end in view whereas we did not, hence

xi

they possessed a *dynamic* with an instrumental "morality" that we failed to produce with a humanitarian morality of ends. The difference in *dynamic* lay in ideology. This is not a claim that these ideologies do not have their various factions, as is now being exhibited in the Sino-Soviet schism, nor is it a claim that all factions have the same world-wide aims, but it is my belief that classic Marxism-Leninism is still the basic source of their inspiration and various interpretations even in the midst of their arguments as to which faction is truly orthodox. Therefore, I shall base my analysis of Marxism-Leninism upon what I consider to be the most vigorous and well-developed aspects of the movement, that which is generally found in Russian communism, with certain relevant elements from the thought of Mao Tse-tung.

The free world still lacks the dynamic ideological balance and clarity necessary to deal with the immoral ideologies; ideologies are as much a fact of this age as atomic energy and are more important because of their capability to manipulate ideas and atomic power as tools and weapons. Therefore, if we are to cope successfully with the immoral ideologies, we shall require (1) a moral force with more *dynamic,* (2) a more efficient use of methodology, and (3) a clear world-view of more humanly noble purpose than is found in the totalitarian ideologies. By whatever name we chose to call this solution, it still amounts to the elimination of wrong ideas and morally inferior ideologies by the use of better ideas in the form of a morally superior ideology.

The totalitarian ideologies have been encouraged by the muddle in the thinking of the free world which expresses itself even in the area of philosophy as a morally static intellectualism, whose offspring has been scientism on the one hand and ivory tower *value-ism* on the other. A number of thinkers have become aware of this inability of contemporary Western ethics to deal with the moral scope (Ap. 8) of the modern ideological conflict, and they have suggested certain characteristics which an adequate moral philosophy must possess. Several prime examples are as follows:

1. Hofstadter proposes that an adequate moral philosophy must itself be accepted as a moral undertaking (Ap. 9 and 10). Laird's position is even bolder in his assertion that persistent moral preparation is necessary not only for moral philosophy but even for a synoptic apprehension of the universe as a whole (Ap. 11).

2. Price proposes that philosophy itself should accept the moral challenge of putting first things first in the light of human need; it must not allow language and terminology to dictate away philosophical content in the form of "questions which ought to be asked" (Ap. 12).

3. Hepburn (Ap. 13), Hofstadter (Ap. 14), and Hill (Ap. 15) apparently agree in supporting the position that an adequate moral philosophy must take account of the data resulting from moral experience, and, according to Hepburn, particularly the experience of morally sensitive people.

4. Bergson (Ap. 16, 17), Braithwaite (10:15–17), and Hill (Ap. 18) hold that an adequate moral philosophy must involve a definite relationship to action (Ap. 19).

5. Price claims an adequate moral philosophy must have a definite relationship to a "unified conceptual scheme" (Ap. 20, 21), which Hill corroborates in other terms by the call for a "new synthesis" (Ap. 22) to answer the "current confusion in contemporary ethical theories" (27:2).

All of these proposals seem to presuppose that there is something lacking in contemporary ethics, with particular emphasis upon Anglo-American writers (Ap. 13); they all suggest a dissatisfaction with the uncommitted philosophical spirit in ethics which leads to intellectualism, scientism, and particularly the radical moral subjectivism of positivism. I believe that all of these thinkers would agree with me concerning the seeming incapacity of Western ethics to raise a barricade of sustained moral action against the ubiquitous forces of disintegration appearing in both totalitarian ideologies and alien ethical systems; the root of their disintegrating powers consists in a manipulative relativism which is antithetical to the ultimate values of both democratic humanitarianism and New Testament Christianity.

Even if some consider it feasible to define 'ethics' in the more narrow intellectualistic fashion of G. E. Moore (68:20), it is my conviction that moral philosophy must accept a broader scope and be able to deal with the moral conflicts between men and nations. To deal on this scale, moral philosophy must have at least as much philosophical breadth as the immoral ideologies and alien ethical systems it encounters. I think this breadth cannot be found outside of the inclusion of a relational approach which forms an essential moral and methodological bridge between the areas of knowing, believing, and doing (Ap. 1). Once we develop the implications of this relational approach in moral philosophy, in order to deal with the threat of the immoral ideologies, it becomes obvious that such an approach implies a strong relationship of moral philosophy to a moral ideology. This moral ideology serves as the necessary bridge between moral theory and moral action. (Moral philosophy is not a moral ideology, even though the two overlap considerably, just as a moral ideology is not mere moral action in spite of a considerable overlapping.) In other words, once we develop a fully relational approach to moral questions by relating (1) knowing-believing (including valuing), (2) believing-doing, and (3) doing-knowing, then we have the three basic elements of an ideology in the sense that (1) knowing-believing is the world-view, (2) believing (valuing) -doing is the *dynamic,* and (3) doing-knowing is the methodology. A well developed ideology must include these three elements, a world-view, a *dynamic,* and a methodology, on the ground that it is an empirical fact that all effective ideologies actually have these elements regardless of how we try to define 'ideology.' Hence, the relational approach by the moral philosopher to knowing, believing, and doing is the development of a conceptual scheme of a moral ideology, just as the relational approach of the practical moralist to knowing, believing, and doing is the actual creation of a moral ideology (Ap. 1); this relation of areas allows moral philosophy to avoid an undue abstractness that is out of touch with the empirical world of our actual moral conflict.

This relational approach implies a moral ideology both schematically and actually, if the relations are vital enough. Furthermore, it includes all of the elements prescribed by the various contemporary philosophers mentioned above; therefore, a philosophical analysis of a moral ideology will demonstrate that the nature of an actual moral ideology is the best schematic framework for the integration of these heretofore disjoined ethical proposals. In fact, my opening chapters will present evidence that this is the solution given by certain contemporary philosophers (for example, Northrop).

Even though I am not philosophically alone in advocating a moral ideology, I am seeking to go beyond the role of an advocate into that of showing what a moral ideology must be, that is, what it must be in order to be both consistent with, and contributive toward, a moral philosophy capable of dealing with the current moral conflict.

Therefore, in order to avoid confusion of purpose in this inquiry, it is first necessary to list what I am *not* seeking to do through my relational approach to moral philosophy.

1. I am not seeking to argue the priority of knowledge or belief; I am contending for their integrated relation in moral philosophy.

2. I am not seeking to argue the primacy of intellect and will, even though I hold that the philosophical interest in the nature of will has been neglected through the domination of the intellectualistic tradition in Western philosophy. I maintain that there is an urgent need for a dynamic relationship between intellect and will in moral philosophy akin to that found in a moral ideology.

3. I am not arguing the extent of verifiable knowledge in the issue of a broad versus a narrow definition of knowledge; I am including data on both types and I show the dangers of both extremes when subjected to ideological manipulation. My definition of 'knowledge' corresponds to that of C. I. Lewis, i.e. it is not a descriptive but a normative category (51:10, 27—31).

4. I am not seeking to argue the primacy of theory or action; an effective and relevant moral philosophy must include a vital synthesis of both in its cognitive scheme, and since a moral ideology is capable of this synthesis it is in that sense related to, and contributive toward, moral philosophy. The challenge of this inquiry is directed just as pointedly to the thinker who believes in the practical role of moral philosophy but does not understand how to effect his practical ideals, as it is directed to the intellectualist who prefers ivory tower ethics. My concern with the relation of action to moral theory is primary only insofar as highly developed forms of practice (for example, ideology) can revitalize and correct ethical theories which have become somewhat inapplicable to the present age.

5. I am not arguing the merits of a metaphysically transcendent approach versus a morally naturalistic and immanent approach to moral philosophy; I propose to show how a relational approach in

moral philosophy to the current moral conflict, similar to that of a moral ideology, would in many cases add vitality, relevance, and even clarity to most of our current moral systems (unless they are reductionistic) regardless of their epistemological and ontological trappings.

6. I am not arguing the objectivity versus the subjectivity of human felt-values and value norms; I do maintain that the objectifying of values within human existence is the joint task of ideology and philosophy. Although philosophy essentially clarifies values and ideology effects them, philosophy needs an ideological laboratory to test its normative conclusions empirically, and ideology needs philosophical clarity to add the effective *dynamic* that cannot exist without true universality.

7. I am not arguing the primacy of the 'right' or the 'good'; I agree with C. I. Lewis that both are necessary but that the 'right' is the major premise of the moral syllogism (52:75, 76).

8. I am not arguing the question of whether moral belief is essentially natural or supernatural; I do believe, however, that a considerable amount of *dynamic* in the moral life is lost unless the supernatural is allowed to be a live philosophical option, particularly where naturalism has failed empirically on the human moral scene. To judge the ethical merits of supernaturalism, a prior question must be solved as to whether supernaturalism is advocated in experiential or metaphysical form. Even though I am not defending the point here, it may help the reader to know that I accept experiential supernaturalism found in certain forms (Biblical), but reject speculative metaphysical (Scholastic, etc.) supernaturalism.

9. I am not arguing the question of illumination versus motivation in moral philosophy; I maintain that both are necessary, but that Western philosophy has allowed its zeal on the side of illumination of moral norms to outrun its concern for the dynamic motivation of sustained action. My proposed relational approach will suggest a definite means of gaining a more reasonable balance between norms and *dynamic,* especially through a study of moral ideology.

10. I am not arguing the question of egoism versus altruism; any non-reductionistic moral system could be enlightened, if not

improved, by a definite relationship to a moral ideology, especially since the heart of the current moral crisis is ideological. I do hold, however, that all forms of egoism, even though they may have some positive effects, are inclined to possess too much "moral friction" for the moral demands of this age (67:134—174).

11. I am not arguing the primacy of ideology or philosophy; even though they overlap considerably they are still different disciplines. However, this entire inquiry is an argument for the interrelatedness of ideology and philosophy, just as man is the interrelation of will and intellect. On the one hand, this need of interrelatedness has been made very obvious by the totalitarian ideologies in their neglect of proper philosophical analysis of their ideological presuppositions and goals; on the other hand, this need of interrelatedness has also been focused by the general inability of Western intellectuals to prevent their scientific and technological advancements from being subverted toward pernicious ends, due to their lack of understanding of the full nature of ideology.

Now that I have delimited my field of inquiry both negatively and positively to the point of showing that my aim is a conceptual analysis of the relation of a moral ideology to dynamic moral philosophy, it is obvious that the current confusion that dogs us must have had its roots somewhere within the history of thought itself. My aim in focusing my subject matter as I have mentioned above rests upon my obvious presupposition that the intellectualistic and scientistic traditions in philosophical ethics have produced the groundwork of much of our present moral sterility, which is most pronounced in positivism and the systems that reflect it. The roots of this problem go back as far as the dawn of Western philosophy itself, centering most consistently in the problem of epistemology.

Epistemology, in its evolution from the early Greek philosophers up to the present, has undergone a general narrowing of its conception of the proper domain of knowledge. Consequently, many of the areas of cognition formerly classed as "knowledge" (metaphysics, religion, pure reason, the *a priori*) are now classed as various areas of belief. Just as the epistemologists have shaved away the less demonstrable forms of cognition from the knowing process, so has a corresponding reductionism been operative in moral philosophy. In some cases this reductionism has benefited moral philosophy by an increase in clarity of meaning; but in others it has robbed moral philosophy of a considerable amount of its normative power and practical effectiveness because it has overlooked the dynamic role of justified belief in its complementary relationship to knowledge.

This inquiry, therefore, will proceed according to the following summary:

Chapter 1: A consideration of the evolution of epistemology since the early Greeks will show how the changing relation of belief to knowledge has had a corresponding effect on moral philosophy, notably in respect to the possibility of a sustained and vital relationship between moral theory and moral action. As epistemology has progressively transferred many of its less demonstrable (but often dynamic) areas over into the vague hinterland of belief, moral philosophy either has found ways to preserve these morally essential elements or has become progressively sterile in human affairs. This sterility has been uniquely prominent in this century (Ap. 23). It is shown how some of the greater philosophers have been able to retain these justified beliefs in a working cooperation with their general epistemologies. Philosophers, like Northrop, affirm that the living embodiment of justified beliefs is to be found in a moral ideology (Ap. 24); a moral ideology by its nature includes the proper commitment to justified belief as well as knowledge as an attitude which is foundational to the morality of survival.

Chapter 2: The word 'ideology' has come to have a considerable diversity of meaning and demands historical treatment. It is used here in its etymological sense, i.e., 'the systematic study and use of ideas' (to which I have added) as tools and weapons for the mobilization of the human will.

Chapter 3: Marxism-Leninism has been chosen for discussion (essentially the Russian version due to the accessibility of its literature) as one prime example of an ideology both because it is relevant to contemporary moral problems and because it has exhibited dynamic success in the mobilization of human will within an "ethical" or normative framework. Its activities show clearly what areas current moral philosophy must deal with on an equally comprehensive and dynamic level. The permanent possession of free inquiry itself may well depend upon our ability to develop a moral force capable of competing successfully with such immoral ideologies as Marxism-Leninism. I hold to the thesis that only a more powerful ideology, or its equivalent by any other name, can defeat a wrong but powerful ideology.

Chapter 4: There must be a description, consequently, of the nature of a moral ideology. A moral ideology has three basic elements: a *dynamic*, a world-view, and a methodology. Its only valid aim is morality, rather than point-of-view (Ap. 25). A moral ideology is essentially united wills in motion through a plan of action.

Chapter 5: A moral ideology has several stabilizing factors which are very necessary to a workable moral philosophy. These stabilizing elements include conscience, absolute norms, the proper balance of language that fosters volitional consistency, and the inclusion of the language of the will. Whereas belief has generally been considered an unstable element in cognition, this chapter shows where it may act in a role which stabilizes germinal premonitions for critical attention.

Chapter 6: Finally, a moral ideology must possess dynamic factors which work in harmony with the best and most universal moral norms. The sources of these *dynamics* are inseparably linked to a clear understanding of the needs of the human will to decide continually, and to decide on the basis of frictionless norms. It is these dynamic factors in the active form of an ideology that serve to test the human applicability of theoretical moral norms. Since it is essentially a complexus of dynamic beliefs, a moral ideology is capable of inspiring man to accept the moral challenge of remaking the world by first accepting change within himself.

It will probably be noticed by the reader, especially since "moral philosophy" is included in the title, that I have not specifically said which ethical position I maintain. Nevertheless, I believe that is not presently essential, since the ideas put forth allow a breadth of choice within an altruistically based framework. It will be obvious that I am not presently seeking to foster one type of ethical theory at the expense of all others, but primarily to show how most theories have neglected certain basic volitional elements, such as those found in world ideologies, to the point of impoverishing themselves. What follows is not an attempt at a systematic exposition of my own ethical theory, but, until such a time when I might possibly write one, the following chapters will include many of my basic ethical ideas in the forms that have been living realities in my own experience. The diagram (Ap. 1) gives a cognitive clue to my ethical position; but, since it is merely a metaphor in visible form, it must not be pressed too hard for any comprehensive rigor.

Special gratitude is due to Professors Wilbur H. Long, William H. Werkmeister, and Walter M. Crittenden for their kind and careful help in reading and making constructive suggestions about the manuscript. Hence, any shortcomings of the ideas and text should be laid to my account.

I am also indebted to the gracious and careful teaching, in my graduate student days, of Emile Cailliet and Clarence Irving Lewis. In these two men I found a spirit of philosophical integrity and humility that encouraged me to try to see the issues of thought in the light of basic assumptions, and to find a philosophical outlook which was adequately comprehensive and harmonious with the best things I have found in life. Although they would likely not find particular interest in some of my own concerns nor express them in the same way if they did have them, it was this magnanimous spirit in both men that inspired considerable impetus in my own efforts to write upon a number of the things as those that will follow and, to me, seem important.

K. Bruce Miller

Los Angeles, Calif.
June, 1969

Chapter 1

A HISTORICAL SURVEY OF JUSTIFIED BELIEF

Using C. I. Lewis's definition of knowledge (Ap. 26) as a norm, my purpose in this chapter will be to show how the evolution of theoretical epistemology toward a generally narrower definition of knowledge has tended toward a leanness of content in moral philosophy; this leanness has been avoided historically by a number of the greater philosophers mentioned below who have refused to reject certain forms of moral cognition (i.e., dynamic beliefs) which would not fit into the stricter, more scientific definitions of knowledge of their era. Those thinkers who have not been interested in, or able to retain, these dynamic beliefs within their moral systems have been the forerunners of a considerable class of contemporary intellectualistic and scientistic thinkers who are unable to give humanity very much that is morally adequate to meet the needs of a confused world that has suddenly been immersed in the age of ideology and atomic power; their leanness lies in a faulty attitude to moral cognition which they could have avoided by accepting the epistemological spirit of some of the greater thinkers mentioned below who were able to give a philosophically noble place to certain forms of dynamic cognition.

The general theory of knowledge, with its increasingly clarified but foreshortened interpretation of the proper domain of knowledge, has had great influence upon conceptions of the nature and domain of moral cognition; consequently, moral cognition in turn has progressively come to be defined more narrowly in a manner closely approximating the situation in speculative epistemology. As the evolution of epistemology has increasingly given philosophers occasion to discard areas that have not been able to establish themselves as being more than belief, moral philosophers similarly have too often come to discard belief itself as a major element in moral cognition. This neglect of belief as a major moral category has had

1

a number of significant consequences, which will be discussed later. For the present we shall consider the evolution of epistemology itself as a basis to interpret the various trends and emphases in moral philosophy, and particularly the contemporary trend to neglect the creative role of belief. Let us follow this evolutionary progression by beginning with the early Greeks.

The Relation of Belief to Knowledge among Traditional Philosophers

The Early Greeks Stress the Object Alone.—The pre-Socratic Greeks were fully optimistic about their belief that knowledge could rightly extend itself into any domain of cognition where a systematic and rational approach was possible (99:25). In their intellectual endeavors, described by Frederick Copleston as "philosophico-scientific activities" (17:21), they saw no real distinction between what we now separate as science and systematic speculation; consequently the pre-Socratics had little or no conscious awareness of how completely belief had infiltrated their essentially dogmatic philosophical outlook. Belief functioned in their cognitive endeavors as an unrecognized psychological factor rather than a consciously acceptable epistemological principle. Copleston claims that this situation in pre-Socratic philosophy was the result of their practically exclusive emphasis upon the external world, that is, "the Object, the not-self" (17:78). Later Greek thinkers began the trend of giving philosophical recognition to the willing and acting subject, but fideism found full development as an explicit cognitive principle only in Christian thought which emphasized inner decision as a principle of enlightenment.

The Sophists Stress the Subject and Recognize Conflicting Beliefs.—Prominence to man, the Subject, was first given by the Sophists whose aim was essentially practical and microcosmic, rather than rationalistic and macrocosmic. Although they gave a considerable place to theory, their knowledge of other nations and their diverse ways of life caused them to be sceptical of the older Greek deductive and rationalistic emphasis. Since, in the words of Zeller, their approach was "empirico-inductive" (99:77), they were alert to the fact that ideas on the same subject differed from

2

one society to another; consequently, they were led to put novel emphasis upon the Subject that wills as well as thinks, which in turn served to raise important questions about the thinker himself. The Sophists on the one hand accepted belief (i.e. that form of cognition left when knowledge was not possible) consciously as their only available means of cognition through their recognition of the limited capacity of the thinking subject to attain knowledge, while, on the other hand, they accepted belief unconsciously in terms of a dogmatically relativistic metaphysics.

Socrates Distinguishes Knowledge from Opinion by Universal Definition.—Socrates was the first of the Greeks, as far as it is known, to state a well-defined position concerning the nature and limitations of knowledge itself (*Euth.,* 293, 297; *Charm.,* 169; *Phaedr.,* 278D). True knowledge, we are told, must begin essentially by self-knowledge (*Apol.,* 38A); and as far as he was concerned, it ended where cosmological speculation and even natural science began (97:11A). His view of knowledge in general about the universe was sceptical, and in this sense he was part of the Sophist tradition. Yet, unlike the Sophists, he challenged all men to turn inwardly to know themselves. He thereby introduced the distinction between belief and knowledge on the basis of subject matter, which was a definite epistemological advance over the Sophist's sceptical, or at least ambiguous, view of the thinking Subject.

It was essentially by example that Socrates showed the difference between knowledge and the less substantial attempts at cognition. By challenging those who were intellectually presumptuous to come to more adequate and universal definitions, he indicated the realms where knowledge could not be extended, at least at the hands of the contemporaries he addressed. In Socrates there existed one of the first thinkers who made a systematically practical attempt to distinguish real knowledge from speculative belief (*Gorg.,* 454). This distinction was basically a moral matter and it was pursued in order to make men better.

Aristotle supported the view that Socrates was primarily concerned with ethical matters (*Meta.,* 987b). According to the *Metaphysics,* "Socrates occupied himself with the excellences of character, and in connection with them became the first to raise the problem of universal definitions" (*Meta.,* 1078b). Through pur-

3

suing these definitions he was able to separate knowledge from un-critical belief; with him begins the evolution of a most valuable distinction which has continued until the present.

In his effort to give the cognitive process proper rigor, however, Socrates did not dispense with all forms of what we moderns class as 'belief.' He believed and invested in the great conviction of the validity of his own search for something that is unconditioned and absolute, which could be grasped by the human mind and also serve as the basic norm for moral conduct. He believed this to be the wise and just power that governs the affairs of the universe (*Apol.*, 28B, 30C, 35D, 40B, 42A).

Socrates was one of the first to elevate belief, in the form of dynamic conviction, to a philosophical level (Ap. 27). This is a form of cognition that demands its validity to be tested by doing as well as by rational contemplation. The obedience of Socrates to his vision, that spoke of his death on the third day (*Crito*, 44), was based on knowledge of what was to be done in contradistinc-tion from the opinions of the many who would have urged him to compromise his principles by an escape. He called his vision 'knowl-edge,' whereas we moderns would call it 'faith.' But in spite of the difference of terms, on the one hand, Socrates gave philosophical dignity to an area of cognition which the intellectualists and sci-entistic thinkers have neglected in their systems to their own moral impoverishment. On the other hand, Socrates, through his prac-tical and dialectical method, purified the cognitive process of much belief that could not stand the test of clear definition and rational justification.

Plato Elevates the Theoretical and Broadens Knowledge.—If Plato was not primarily the practical moralist that Socrates was, he was not a mere theoretician in his moral philosophy. On the contrary his ethical writings deal with the question of "how to live": both the *Republic* and the *Laws* were written with the pur-pose of being applied, and stress the thesis that the making of good men and the good state are inseparably linked together. Plato preserved and elaborated the basic contribution of Socrates by maintaining that certain kinds of subject matter, relative to their being, are knowledge and certain others are opinion (*Rep.*, 476—478), although he was also careful to distinguish between 'mere'

4

and 'true' opinion (*Sym.*, 202). He also agreed with Socrates on the central position of moral philosophy in human thinking; however, around this exalted center he established a number of lower levels of cognition which, with reference to his useful image of the divided line (*Rep.*, 509), might be said to resemble a dime concentrically stacked upon a quarter and a half-dollar. The dime represents, so to speak, the higher focus of the Good which is grasped by dialectical reason; the quarter, understanding; the half-dollar, faith or conviction; the broad and undifferentiated expanse of the table represents the perception of shadows (*Rep.*, 513).

Due to his broader notion of the nature of knowledge than that of Socrates, Plato's epistemology involved a wider distinction between theory and practice, a distinction which Socrates overlooked when he proposed that moral knowledge was the only knowledge. Philosophy, in Plato's estimation, did not limit itself in content to the thinking subject; hence, the extensiveness of the world of knowable entities gave new and revolutionary dignity to purely theoretical contemplation in the guidance of the good life. At the same time this broadness gave proper balance to the other end of the human scale by the novel recognition of the role of moral opinions (true beliefs) in the ethical lives of the masses.

Plato's broader epistemological framework (*Rep.*, 509) led to a new trend in which cognition theory began to set the pattern for moral knowledge. Fortunately this did not result in a reductionism in the method of moral cognition, because Plato made the Idea of the Good central in all cognitive matters. He says,

> Now, that which imparts truth to the known and the power of knowing to the knower is what I would have you term the idea of good, and this you will deem to be the cause of science, and of truth in so far as the latter becomes the subject of knowledge; . . . (*Rep.*, 508)

Later thinkers, who made matters other than the Good cognitively central, could not with equal justification follow Plato's trend of allowing epistemology to dominate the method and content of moral cognition. Where this has been the case, moral philosophy has become increasingly theoretical and rationalistic in a purely speculative sense (Ap. 28).

Plato's chief contribution to ethical history was his purpose to distinguish the knowledge-worthy from the belief-worthy, and both of these from idle speculation. Unfortunately, if this delineating of spheres has been an asset to later epistemology, as an aid to distinguish the volitional from the intellectual, it has also tended to pauperize ethics among lesser thinkers who have not made a special effort to enrich moral philosophy by other means.

Aristotle Decentralizes Ethics by Centralizing Substance.—By a change in the primary focus of epistemology from the Platonic Idea of the Good to substance, Aristotle played a major role in down-grading ethics on the cognitive scale from the pinnacle of theoretic centrality to the level of a systematic, practical skill. In stressing this principle in the *Categoriae,* it is said that,

> . . . primary substances are most properly called substances in virtue of the fact that they are the entities which underlie everything else, and that everything else is predicated of them or present in them. (2b)

The idea of the good, in Aristotle's system, is not a substance but is rather a universal property *(Meta.,* 1039a). Having in his metaphysics a less exalted and crucial status than substance, the idea of the good comes to play a cognitively lesser role in Aristotle's epistemology than in the Platonic scheme. As Aristotle departed from Plato in his metaphysics of general cognition by refusing to make the Good theoretically central *(Nic. Eth.,* 1096, 1097), he consequently had an even greater reason to do this in the area of moral cognition, because of the practical unattainability of the Platonic Idea of the Good. The metaphysics of Aristotle's cognitive system had dissolved the Good into innumerable goods, each within the reach of particular living men.

Aristotle made a new and wider distinction between science and ethics when, contrary to Plato, he laid claim to infallibility in physics and metaphysics, and when he reduced ethics to the level of probability. This shift was associated with his identification of epistemology with the knowledge of causes. Exact knowledge is to know the cause (s) of a thing and to know that the fact could not be otherwise than what it is, that every connection between a singular existence and its causes is a necessary one *(Anal. Post.,* 71b).

6

In the Peripatetic system, ethics differs from pure science because it studies what ought to be rather than what is the case, and because it deals with the contingent rather than the necessary. Not only is it incapable of the rigid demonstration possessed by scientific knowledge, its principles and data do not permit infallible generalization. Consequently, it is a practical endeavor based largely upon common sense. In the *Nicomachean Ethics* Aristotle asserts:

> Since, then, the present inquiry does not aim at theoretical knowledge like the others (for we are inquiring not in order to know what virtue is, but in order to become good, since otherwise our inquiry would have been of no use), we must examine the nature of actions, namely how we ought to do them; for these determine also the nature of the states of character that are produced, as we have said. Now, that we must act according to the right rule is a common principle and must be assumed . . . (1103b)

Contrary to the methodology of science, the knowledge of the Good, and hence the good life, which was so dominantly central in Plato, is identified in Aristotle's system with Plato's third level down on the divided line. Or, perhaps, more accurately, it is an entirely different sphere, in which rigid demonstration is not the criterion of the value of a discipline.

The empiricistic elements of Aristotle's theory of knowledge also tended to separate his position from those held by Socrates and Plato. Whereas Socrates seems to have identified the good life with the quest for adequate and universal definitions, and Plato identified it with the metaphysical quest for the Universal Good, Aristotle stressed the particular fact as that which gave moral enlightenment. His empiricism led him to stress the question of proper means (*Nic. Eth.*, 1144a) or the way in which ethics seeks to make men good, one important means being the empirical observation of particular good men in the light of particular moral issues. This was a contribution that Plato failed to see as valuable, but which is still relevant today (7:50).

Although moral cognition, according to Aristotle, was not dignified by the name 'science' (*episteme*), the study of the good life was nevertheless a systematic discipline. Yet in spite of his personal sense of the importance of moral philosophy, this exclusion of ethics from the realm of exact knowledge gave added emphasis to the psychological and metaphysical tendency in Western thought, suggested earlier by Democritus and Protagoras, to reduce moral cognition to a secondary level among philosophical disciplines. The Scholastic tradition seized upon Aristotle's naturalistic approach to ethics (instead of recognizing the full measure of their Apostolic heritage) and thereby became a prominent historical perpetrator of the moral and spiritual poverty which has plagued Western theological and secular ethics to this day. Aristotle's chief contribution was one of indicating the difference between the methods of science and those of ethics. But since he did not class ethics among the exact sciences, he failed to show how to maintain the psychological and ontological importance of moral cognition, in spite of its cognitive differences, within the whole of a philosophical framework.

Apostolic Christian Thought Adds Dynamic Elements of Cognition to Epistemology.—Christian thought added a new dimension to the subject of epistemology by stressing the factor of will as it is manifested in decision. For the first time in the West, Biblical teaching made it clear that certain intellectual questions can be clarified only on the basis of prior decision. When the fishermen sought to find out if Jesus was the Messiah by asking him, "Where are you staying?," he answered by the call for the decision to follow him in order to find out (John 1:38, 39). This approach to enlightenment through action was amplified by the statement of Jesus, "If any man's will [decision] is to do his [God's] will, he shall know whether the teaching is from God or whether I am speaking on my own authority" (John 7:17). The point is that the more profound types of spiritual and moral understanding do not exist in a volitional vacuum.

Apostolic Christianity had no academic philosophy like the Greeks, but its epistemology may be compared with that of Hellenism by the cognitive innovations it introduced which centered in the will and decision. These new cognitive elements are *agape,* revelation, faith, human dignity, righteousness, responsibility, free will, sin; in a highly developed form, all these were foreign to Greek thought.

8

Plato and Aristotle held that a man's action was the result of the promptings of his character, which was the sum total of his natural gifts as developed by his particular moral education. From this position the main problem in ethics was one of determining which natural or acquired traits were the best and how they were to be instilled or evoked. On their principles, representative of Greek tradition, it was difficult to distinguish between the moral virtues and such other virtues as beauty, charm, intelligence and health. Lack of clarity on this distinction led the Greeks to an aristocratic ethical outlook, according to which the best life can be attained only by the fortunate few who possess high birth, wealth, education, and leisure to contemplate.

The Christian tradition, on the other hand, held that a man may do his duty to the highest regardless of his outward circumstances of wealth, education or birth. It linked this moral excellence with a new level of cognition in the concept of a responsibility and a freedom of the will not essentially determined by heredity and environment. Men could choose to do wrong knowing it to be so, and they could feel remorse and allot blame; whereas the Greeks considered that they could do little more than feel regret and express their distaste of certain actions (100).

The aim of both Greek and Christian ethics was to make men good, although between them were basic differences profoundly influenced by their respective ideas of the theory of knowledge. The early Christians accepted most of the significant ethical ideas of the Greeks, yet they possessed unique principles: they added the factor of revelation as a very substantial type of cognition or 'knowledge,' and believed any type of man could become good. Their dynamic concepts, mentioned above, of revelation, responsibility, *agape,* free will, sin, faith, etc. were the key to the difference between the two traditions. But it was not long before the two merged philosophically and the Greek spirit of intellectualism began to dominate.

After Augustine the Greek concept of knowledge overshadowed these dynamic elements, yet their spirit was preserved by men like St. Francis of Assisi and later reinstated by Luther and others. Kant gave the Christian element of freedom (which was approximated by the Stoics) a central position of philosophical dignity. Although

9

the other elements are still awaiting more adequate examination by non-theological thinkers, the immoral ideologies have already used them to considerable advantage in perverted but considerably dynamic forms.

The spirit of Scholasticism buried dynamic forms of cognition even though it discussed them in the abstract. (Modern moral philosophy is not markedly different except for its secular orientation.) But, a new philosophical spirit began with Nominalism and found a great breakthrough in Locke.

The Effect of Scientific Methodology upon Moral Philosophy

Locke's Moral and Methodological Balance.—Locke is, in one basic sense, the leading spirit of modern scientific empiricism, even though men like Bacon helped to introduce the empirical method. Between 1671 and 1690, he switched his emphasis from philosophical subject matter to methodology (48:74). Along with Descartes, Locke was one of the first to give extreme prominence to the question of how we know what we (think) we know. In fact, it was Locke's works which have been instrumental in giving epistemology its present status as a major philosophical discipline. As epistemology has progressed since Locke, one may discover two different approaches to philosophical analysis: the one stresses subject matter (concrete things) ; the other, methodology. This difference of approach presents an interesting problem; the decision to emphasize, either methodology on the one hand, or concrete content on the other, has the possibility of leading to mutually exclusive conclusions from the same data, even though this difference of conclusion is not a necessary result (Ap. 29). Locke attained a desirable balance between these two emphases which was, no doubt, tempered strongly by his own personal commitment to the moral needs of man in the knowing process. A classic example of unbalanced empiricism is to be found in Condillac's sensationism (16:236) ; in contemporary times it is found in logical empiricism, in certain behavioristic forms of new realism, and in the approaches where scientism dominates foundational concepts.

Some of Locke's empiricistic imitators were unaware that the basic purpose of Locke's published writings was inspired in the setting of the struggle for overcoming the barriers of intellectual, religious, and civil liberties. Locke refused to let his methodological analysis dominate him even though he had initiated a new level of importance for methodology. He possessed enough moral wisdom to maintain a state of cognitive balance between his epistemological methodology and his moral subject matter. In fact he says, "I may conclude, that morality is the proper science and business of mankind in general, . . ." (*Essay,* Bk. IV, Ch. XII, Sec. 11). This judgment, however, has not been accepted by many of Locke's alleged followers in the great empirical tradition, who have been insensitive to the central epistemological role of moral cognition. Locke maintained his philosophical balance between the scientific and the moral by (1) showing the limitations of scientific knowledge, and (2) elevating moral cognition to the level of demonstrative certitude equal to that of mathematics (*Essay,* Bk. IV, Ch. IV, Sec. 7). The empirical tradition, since Locke, has continued its development of the first, but has been generally negligent in creating an adequate cognitive substitute for the second. Therefore, even if Locke's method of establishing the certitude of moral cognition is not acceptable to contemporary thinkers, this does not mean that his efforts at maintaining a cognitive balance were unjustified, particularly since these efforts were foundational to free inquiry and liberal democracy.

Hume's Treatment of Justified Belief.—By the time of Hume, Newtonian science and Locke had already given epistemology considerable criteria by which to judge its own limitations; this resulted in a marked narrowing of the domain of what could rightly be called demonstrable knowledge. Descartes' standard of clearness and distinctness and the new respect for mathematics had narrowed the proper domain of knowledge by its exclusion of secondary qualities and certain forms of speculative metaphysics, for example, Greek and Scholastic cosmology and all of Aristotle's causes except efficient cause. But even though Galilean-Cartesian-Newtonian science had made a clean but increasingly narrowed channel of knowledge by eliminating the qualitative from science, Hume now questioned the demonstrability of science's assumption of efficient

11

causality, and was consequently led to emphasize the subjective belief-factor in science; thereby he shifted the basic foundations of science from empirical physics to psychological anthropology. Objectively this led to the question of belief, subjectively to that of moral principles and values since the foundation of physics itself came from the inner man. This encouraged subsequent positivistic and reductionistic trends, which have restricted the field of knowledge and have consigned other types of cognition to the vague and unrespectable hinterland of uncritical belief. Hume himself did this with the Christian faith, but he was still sensible enough not to commit this folly against moral philosophy, as his contemporary positivistic followers have done. When he saw that moral cognition did not properly fit within a purely mathematico-scientific framework, he gave the moral realm a position of cognitive, and even scientific, centrality, the understanding of which was dependent upon the thinker's acumen and "the science of mind" (35:xix).

The great contribution of Hume to our modern opinions about moral cognition was that he challenged the intellectualists to consider the importance of creating order in the hinterland of our beliefs and values and by showing the strict and narrow boundaries of the channel of verifiable knowledge. His methodological rule, that none of the arts and sciences "can go beyond experience" (35:xxi), gave a renewed orderliness and purity in the realm of justified belief similar to the orderliness Newton brought to science. In other words, the historical picture now began to assume a new perspective in which the landscape of belief, beside the ever-narrowing channel of verifiable knowledge, proceeds to take on a much more important role than formerly recognized. Hume showed us that a thorough study of human nature reveals that man must chart his way through life by his beliefs and values as well as by intellectually verified knowledge, of which there is very little. He also emphasized that belief involves definite "feeling" or conviction and differs from mere conception or imagination. Hume says,

> ... the difference between fiction and belief lies in some sentiment or feeling, which is annexed to the latter, not to the former, and which depends not on the will, nor can be commanded at please. (34:48)

Whether Hume was successful or not in his efforts to determine which beliefs were justified, he is at least to be commended for his effort to show the nature of justified belief, which lies between the channel of scientific knowledge on the one hand, the slough of idle speculation on the other. Here he laid the groundwork for Kant to make room for faith on a logical basis.

Kant Elevates Moral Cognition.—Kant was probably the first philosopher of modern times to make a thorough inquiry into both the nature of theoretically necessary beliefs of "practical reason" and of "pure reason" with its "transcendental ideas," through which alone our understanding can come into "completeness and synthetical unity" (42:116). These practical and transcendental beliefs, however, are distinguished from speculation in that they are not limited to any one person's private experience but represent "experience as a whole" (42:116).

In his "Orientation in Thinking" Kant suggested an important distinction by separating speculative belief from the realm of "rational belief" (39:300). Human reason itself has certain subjective needs, hence it must presuppose such concepts as "a First Being as the supreme intelligence and highest good" (39:297). This fulfills man's rational need "to make the concept of the unlimited the basis of limited things and thus of all other things; . . ." (39:300).

Furthermore, Kant was careful to show the distinction between the two types of "rational belief." The first deals with the needs of reason as an hypothesis of pure reason (based upon subjective grounds) which can never be converted into knowledge. The second type of "rational belief" is a postulate of reason which fulfills reason's need in the practical sense, not because it answers all the logical requirements of certainty, but because it is not inferior in degree to any type of cognition, even though it is completely different (39:300, 301). Kant showed how the practical use of reason is even more important than the theoretical use (Ap. 30). At this point he (probably unwittingly) created the philosophical groundwork for ideological philosophy by giving the criteria by which human reason must make certain assumptions. Yet he showed how belief may be fully consistent and cooperative with the highest use of knowledge (Ap. 31).

Kant has further changed the philosophical landscape of Hume,

13

Locke, and Aristotle by dividing cognition into the two distinct streams of scientific understanding and moral reasoning. By his destruction of pure reason as a source of ontological knowledge, he made the channel of theoretical cognition even narrower; but he rebalanced the situation by a new re-emphasis on the role of will in philosophy that had been scarce since Augustine. Kant put back into philosophy what the reformers, like Luther, put back into society. He considered that his mission was to make room for faith and he made a most noble effort to demonstrate that there are certain areas where the moral disposition can never fall into unbelief (39:14, 247).

Modern Cognitive Theory and Moral Philosophy.—In this century moral philosophy has been profoundly affected both positively and negatively through the narrowing of the scope of general knowledge, a narrowing which has resulted from the loss of the *a priori* as a form of scientific truth (96:207) and the general scepticism concerning practically all types of non-verifiable cognition. The positivists have made further semi-successful attempts to limit knowledge to a clean but narrow channel in their rejection of norms and values as forms of meaningful cognition; this has had a stultifying effect upon contemporary ethics.

The quantitative exactness of science has become fascinating to certain philosophers who have extended its principles to cover ethical questions. In contemporary ethics this trend had gone to its extreme in the logical empiricists and in those who feel that the ethical philosopher is limited to the analysis of words and moral language. To them exactness in the realm of knowledge is paramount, even at the cost of becoming trivial; and they maintain that these trivialities are legitimate in moral philosophy. Granting that what they have done has at least been instructive and has added to the clarifying of certain problems, it is nonetheless obvious that to retreat deeply into the meta-ethical realm is to make moral philosophy completely insignificant in human life. If contemporary definitions of the limits of knowledge in general rightly delimit the cognitive factors in ethics, then philosophy must find some other way of dealing with these extra-knowledge factors which are 'beliefs.' These active beliefs, which traditional philosophers considered to be some sort of legitimate cognition, are neither scientific knowledge (at least not yet) nor are they mere emotions as Ayer claims (3:107).

Keeping in mind the modern conceptions of knowledge, based upon the innovations and added technical sharpness of contemporary epistemology, it is the central hypothesis of this chapter that the relational balance between knowledge and justified belief must be restored (Ap. 32) in order to deal properly with the current problems in the areas of social, moral and political life. Although this balance has not yet occurred throughout Western philosophy in general, however, it has been maintained to an extent in the writings of the contemporary philosophers to be treated in the remainder of this chapter.

Belief as an Essential Form of Cognition in Contemporary Philosophers

It is obvious that the great innovators in both science and ethics have been men of considerable belief or faith of some sort, a belief which used (as optimism uses technology for human betterment) and cooperated with knowledge rather than a belief which had no relevance to it; the more discerning moral thinkers recognize this.

Bergson's Dynamic Belief.—Although the area of belief has been inadequately treated, it has not been totally neglected in contemporary moral philosophy. One of the best examples is Bergson's case that the open or dynamic type of morality involves various types of what should rightly be called belief (7:44, 47, 61, 77). His ideas will be treated at length later.

Dewey's Hypothetical Beliefs.—Dewey labels belief a 'hypothesis.' He claims that there are no self-evident or universally valid rules of conduct (I do not agree with the spirit of this); moral rules are hypotheses which have been found to work in many cases and hence offer helpful suggestions; they offer no more. Dewey is partly right when he claims that moral rules are hypotheses (a type of belief) but he is not right in saying that that is all they are (21:277).

Prichard's Ethical Beliefs.—Prichard gives the problem of belief in moral philosophy a significant hearing. He was able to per-

15

suade Ross to accept the view that one's duty does not depend upon the situation as it actually is, but upon what one believes. Ross had claimed that it was our duty to bring to pass the state of affairs which would satisfy the most stringent obligations upon us. Prichard convinced Ross that such a state of affairs may be beyond one's knowledge or ability, 'ought' implies 'can,' and the best we can do is to make an honest effort to produce the state of affairs which we believe fitting to the circumstances, as we believe them to be. If the state of affairs does not come about through no fault of our own, then we may still claim to have done our duty (83:37, 38; 85:148—156).

Lewis's Perceptive Beliefs.—C. I. Lewis says,

> Any knowing must include belief in something not sense-given but credited as authentic. . . . Perception involves both seeing (or otherwise sensing) and believing. It is the believing which is cognitive; and the believing is inferential in significance . . . Without the affirmation of a belief, there is no inference: . . . It is, indeed, plausible that the guidance of our conduct represents the vital function of belief, . . . (52:26, 28, 42)

Lewis is the contemporary philosopher who, in my estimation, has done as much as anyone to demonstrate the vital role of belief in proper relation to verifiable knowledge. His ideas have a wealth of implications for future development in this area, and particularly in the area of moral cognition.

The Present Problem of Belief.—Lewis has stated the problem and domain of ethics very well. He is in basic sympathy with the great traditional ethical philosophers in conceding that ethics does deal with "what we do" (52:39). The problem now is that, if we would let ethics deal with matters that are centrally significant to life, we must not only deal with what the scientific tradition calls knowledge but also with belief. Thus it is here proposed that the problem of belief be treated and analyzed in keeping with its own unique nature. Any comprehensive study of the nature of belief would have to include the many different shades of belief like the colors of a spectrum from the cool ultra-violet hypotheses of the theoretical physicist to the intense infra-red beliefs of the prophet. Such a complete study of belief, however, would be too vast to

16

cover in any one book, in that it is possibly even greater in scope than the field of knowledge itself. Thus it will be necessary to choose the type of belief which best displays its unique contribution to the realm of moral philosophy. It is my conviction that the area of ideological belief will be the most appropriate to demonstrate belief's unique and necessary contribution to morals, that is, its *dynamism*. Without this dynamic element moral philosophy remains no more than an academic game. It will be only through such a study of the dynamic side of the moral life that the great gap between our ethical theories and the way we actually live may be narrowed. If this is not a significant problem for moral philosophy, then what is?

Ideology, the Form of Justified Belief
Most Capable of Dealing with the Current Conflict
between Men and Nations

The issue at stake is whether our current epistemological balance between the descriptive and the normative is contributive to moral philosophy in a manner that enables it to deal with the moral conflicts between men and nations. This chapter has shown how the greater philosophers have generally been able to retain the belief-worthy within their epistemological systems in spite of its distinction from strict knowledge. But in our own generation, there is probably the greatest need in man's history to re-balance our knowledge-belief (descriptive-normative) spectrum because the current quasi-scholastic trend makes moral philosophy a theoretical game, which is exemplified especially by the logical positivists (22: 6, 23) and those who have been influenced or intimidated by them to retreat out of the philosophical arena of man's actual moral need. Whereas this quasi-scholastic game-playing with moral questions may have been merely an oddity peculiar to intellectualists in former generations, there are two new moral factors in this generation which throw it open to the pernicious manipulation of alien systems unfriendly to the preservation of free inquiry. These two morally ponderous elements are mentioned by F. S. C. Northrop as the first two of three elements that he thinks make our contemporary world unique.

> Three things make the contemporary world unique. The
> first is the release of atomic energy. The second is the ines-
> capably ideological character of its international and do-
> mestic problems. The third is the shift of the center of world
> politics from Western Europe toward Asia. (76)

The first of these two aspects, the release of atomic energy, considered in its moral significance, is inseparably linked with the second factor, the inescapably ideological (Ap. 33) character of our
international and domestic problems. It is not difficult to see that
both the use of atomic power for good or evil and the shift of world
politics will be determined by ideas or ideology.

Therefore, an essential part of both a balanced epistemology
and the morality of survival is an understanding of ideology. There
has been a considerable lack of real clarity about the nature of
ideology especially among intellectualists who have frequently sub-
stituted a somewhat emotional reaction for real analysis of moral
factors that Northrop says are inescapably ideological (Ap. 34, 35).
This is the same trend as where the intellectualists of former times
have rejected new moral data rather than to revise their basic
categories of general cognition.

Let us consider Northrop's proposed beginning of a solution to
world tensions as it shows the necessity of understanding ideology
on a philosophical moral level. He says,

> It is difficult to regard anything as much more important.
> In an atomic age we either understand and transcend the
> different ideologies of the world or we perish. . . . It is im-
> perative therefore if free inquiry is to be allowed the chance
> and the time to understand the diverse ideologies of the world
> and to construct out of them the truly world ideology neces-
> sary to define the common principles for settling interna-
> tional disputes by recourse to law rather than to force, that
> the non-communist ideologies of the world be implemented
> with all the matter and might possible. (Ap. 36)

Northrop's statement, "In an atomic age we either understand and
transcend the different ideologies of the world or we perish," is an
essential matter for moral philosophy. It is in itself an ideological
(i.e. centered in belief and action) statement that, by its nature,
cannot be epistemologically proved unless we are willing to perish

18

to find out. His proposal is to construct a better ideology which is truly world-wide in its scope, a proposal which is also ideological in nature; yet it has some essentially experiental elements in its presuppositions. For example, in world politics many leaders, in agreement with Northrop, are now saying that from their experience the only way to defeat a false or immoral ideology is to give a better one. This is based on the premise that we have found no means of force that will wipe out wrong ideas, except the epistemological factor of better and more consistent ideas (Ap. 37).

One reason why the word 'ideology' has been both unpopular and somewhat confused in its usage is because the communists have used it in a manner which both adds to, and detracts from, its status. More will be said about this in the next two chapters. For the present it is sufficient to say that the contemporay communists usually think of ideology as their basic means of undermining the foundational beliefs or world-view of their enemies.

It must be remembered that Marxism and its modern derivatives are very much of a philosophical fact, even if they are bad philosophies and in spite of their various ideological fronts. Particularly if they are a corrupting epistemological influence to free inquiry and a threat to philosophical freedom, it seems that Northrop may be right in his suggestion that presenting a better, more consistent ideology is the best and only answer. The heart of this lies in a re-balance of our epistemology so as to include the active role of norms and beliefs in a manner capable of dealing with normative systems like Marxism-Leninism that have neglected the proper role of facts.

All through the history of philosophy, the nature of ideas has been a basic and central issue. The nature and scope of ideology is no less an epistemological matter of the nature of ideas than its historical counterparts. The essential difference is that ideas have now become powerful (30:315, 316) tools and weapons in many of their systematic formulations. In fact ideas and the study of their nature can now be put upon an experimental basis more easily in the relational and wholistic context of ideology than if they are approached in a disjointed and atomic fashion. There is as much epistemological difference between a wholistic manifestation of ideas and a series of atomic and disjointed ideas as a fine building is different

19

from a pile of building materials. The Marxist-Leninists have demonstrated this in their highly developed revolutionary techniques.

Therefore, the nature of ideology is broad and important enough to demand philosophical treatment and empirical enough to allow considerable non-metaphysical systematization. It is so thoroughly bound up with germinal moral concepts that moral philosophy cannot afford to neglect it. And it has proved itself to be such a powerful force in the contemporary world that we are forced to compete with even its immoral irrationalism (where such is the case) by a better system of ideas or ideology. At least we will have to compete on this level until we find something to take the place of ideas (Ap. 38). To date no better alternative than Northrop's suggestion of giving a better ideology has appeared on the philosophical scene.

CHAPTER 2

THE ORIGIN AND HISTORICAL DEVELOPMENT OF 'IDEOLOGY'

The Modern Definition of the Word 'Idea' as the Foundation of Ideology and Its Subsequent Definition

Descartes' Notion of the Nature of 'Idea'.—The origin and development of the word 'ideology' had very specific roots in certain modern notions of the nature of ideas. Although 'idea' had been used extensively since the time of Plato as both an ontological and epistemological term, Descartes' modern definition of it (Ap. 39), identified with a nominalistic and subjectivistic account of the knowing process, marked a radical change in which philosophy itself began to shift from the ancient and medieval emphasis upon the outward drama of the universe to an essentially methodological focus upon the inward drama of the soul as the foundation of human cognition (95:202). Descartes was the link of transition between the Greek and Scholastic notion of the immediacy of knowledge in the form of *episteme* (infallibilistic science) and the modern notion of knowledge, according to which there is no direct contact between the mind and the outer world (fallibilism); he was thereby in both camps partially, but in neither camp fully, because of his middle position of rationalistic dependence upon God to establish the certitude of cognition about the external world.

Descartes effected this transition from the medieval to the modern by his epistemological dualism, that an idea "at no time exists outside the mind" (20:10), and its objective referent (for example, an extended body) is completely distinct from the mind. His methodology had no fool-proof means to ensure the truth except his criteria of clearness and distinctness (Ap. 40) and theological optimism. Nevertheless, this did not concern Descartes nearly so much as it would have concerned later thinkers who did not share his

21

strong Scholastic presupposition that the mind has a natural capacity for truth.

Cartesian epistemological dualism and subjectivity (not psychological subjectivism) have had a profound effect upon nearly all subsequent philosophy. His stress upon the "I think therefore I am" as the foundation of cognition has put the thinking self rather than the outward world in the center of the philosophical picture, and has given philosophy the new direction of moving from self-consciousness outward. Henceforth, other selves and the world of objects could not be taken for granted, as in the classical tradition; most of the greater philosophers since Descartes' time have, in one way or another, treated this as a central problem.

Although Descartes sought to save his subjectivistic system from pure scepticism by his appeal to a combination of the geometrical method and the faithfulness of God not to deceive us (19:172), most subsequent philosophers have been unable to take his rationalistic methodology very seriously even though they have generally recognized the importance of his stress upon the thinking subject. They have found it necessary to grapple with the problem of linking the thinker and the external world on a much broader and more relational basis which is particularly exemplified in the philosophies of Kant and Hegel. Kant's transcendental idealism showed his respect for the role of the subject in the thinking process through his copernican revolution in thought; he thereby entered the door that Descartes merely opened, in his stress upon the relational role that moral will and justified belief play in the cognitive process. Hegel's dialectical idealism recognized the contribution of Descartes' epistemological subjectivity to modern philosophy through his own extensive efforts in developing the progress of Spirit on a relational basis (for example, through his dialectic) to the point of a world ideology (Ap. 1).

Although Descartes did not aim at a voluntaristic, and more specifically ideological, philosophy, he definitely opened the door for the emergence of the philosophies foundational to ideology which gave the will and justified belief a prominent role in the cognitive process. Descartes' epistemological subject-centeredness did include the will as a distinct part of the soul (i.e., the thinking being) and thereby prompted a renewed emphasis upon activism in the knowing process, since the term 'idea' signifies the act of cognizing in the knower and not the object of awareness (90:149n). Therefore Descartes encouraged voluntaristic elements in two ways. The first was his unwitting but negative influence upon later thinkers who agreed with him that the knower is limited to his own ideas of the external world, although these thinkers deemed it philosophically unwise either to depend upon Descartes' rationalistic faith in the geometrical method or upon his cognitive claim that God would not deceive us. The second was through his mild epistemological activism in his new conception of the nature of ideas; this was the beginning of a philosophical voluntarism which progressed through Locke's common sense, Hume's ideas of association, and Kant's idea of practical reason to become foundational in different ways to the notions of the nature of ideas central in later ideological philosophies.

Locke's Notion of the Nature of 'Idea'.—Locke's conception of the nature of human ideas influenced his notions of the limitations of knowledge; his stricter (empiricistic) and more limited conception of knowledge necessitated common sense and justified belief in order to do one's duty in the world. Consequently, the need of action upon ideas which were often only probable gave rise to the pragmatical and hence the ideological usage of ideas.

More than any major philosopher up to his time, Locke divested ideas of their Platonic connotation by denying them the status of an eternally existing pattern, or archetype of any class of things. Locke's epistemological dualism (Cartesian) limited ideas to the knowing mind:

> Since the mind, in all its thoughts and reasonings, hath no other immediate object but its own ideas, which it alone does or can contemplate, it is evident that our knowledge is only conversant about them. (*Essay*, Bk. IV, Ch. I, Sec. 1)

Locke referred to an 'idea' as,

> that term which, I think, serves best to stand for whatsoever is the object of the understanding when a man thinks, I have used it to express whatever is meant by phantasm, notion, species, or whatever it is which the mind can be employed about in thinking; . . . (*Essay*, Introd., Sec. 8)

23

Although ideas were, in Locke's estimation, synonymous with all objects of consciousness, they were not identified with 'knowledge.' Ideas are the elements of mental propositions which may be classed either as knowledge, or probability, depending upon their degree of certainty. Ideas can neither be true nor false, certain nor uncertain, since they are not knowledge but only the particular parts that must be combined by reason to form a mental proposition.

Even though it is limited to one's own ideas, knowledge requires more than the mere compounding of simple ideas, because it consists of a seen relation between them. Knowledge must be sure, and thereby it must be constituted by ideas perceived under particular relations that beget assurance of their own necessary connection. Locke claims,

> Knowledge then seems to me to be nothing but the perception of the connexion of and agreement, or disagreement and repugnancy of any of our ideas. In this alone it consists. (*Essay*, Bk. IV, Ch. I, Sec. 2)

This perception of certainty necessary for knowledge may be either an intuitive, a demonstrative, or a sensory perception. Nonetheless, the extent of our knowledge comes short not only of the reality of things, but even of the extent of our own ideas. The knowledge that Locke held to be available concerned one's own existence by intuition, God's existence by demonstration, and the existence of other things by sensation (*Essay*, Bk. IV, Ch. IX—XI). Although, when Locke speaks about the extent of human knowledge (*Essay*, Bk. IV, Ch. III), he gives certitude an extremely narrow berth (*Essay*, Bk. IV, Ch. III, Sec. 22). In fact, he says that our ignorance is infinitely larger than our knowledge (*Essay*, Bk. IV, Ch. III, Sec. 22).

The extent of human knowledge in Locke's estimation is more limited than that of either the Scholastics or Descartes. Since we have no ideas about final realities (for example, Aristotelian final cause), certain knowledge of these things is impossible because there is nothing on which to base perception of agreement or disagreement. But even if the human faculties are not capable of attaining certitude in many areas where the rationalistic metaphy-

24

sicians chose to speculate, Locke held that we do have the necessary faculties

> to discover enough in the creatures to lead us to the knowledge of the Creator, and the knowledge of our duty; and we are fitted well enough with abilities to provide for the conveniences of living: these are our business in this world. (*Essay*, Bk. II, Ch. XXIII, Sec. 12)

Locke maintained that men should seek truth for the end for which God designed it, "which is not as an improvement of their parts and speculations" but moreover for the motive of love for God and their neighbor, using knowledge as a means to make their lives better (58:281).

Locke's emphasis upon common sense, or what we might call action in the form of justified belief, put him among the contributors to the epistemological foundations of the better side of ideological philosophy. With his disdain for enthusiasm it is highly unlikely that Locke would have approved of the way French sensationists, for example, Destutt de Tracy and Condillac, twisted his empiricism toward certain ideological ends; but he made very definite contributions to ideology on two levels. The first was the negative contribution of doing more than any man up to his time in destroying the anti-practical intellectualism of Greek and Scholastic epistemology which had belittled the volitional role of ideas until the 17th century; he helped to destroy this intellectualism by showing the need of common sense and justified belief both because of the limitations of absolute knowledge and because of the necessity of action (*Essay*, Bk. II, Ch. XXI, Sec. 23). The second was the positive contribution of removing 'idea' (with the previous help of Descartes) from its essentially transcendent role, giving many subsequent thinkers a free philosophical conscience in which to treat ideas on a much fuller practical level. In fact his epistemological treatment of the nature of ideas was itself the groundwork for the launching of his practical attack on the absolutism of the Monarchy. Hence his epistemology, even though it narrowed the scope of absolute knowledge, broadened the use of ideas on the practical level even to the point of an ideology. Locke's contribution to practical ideology was shown both in his philosophical justification for a plan of action for deposing an unfit ruler through an orderly revolution (59:433) and in his extensive formulation of the democratic ideology (Ap. 41) which is still dominant in English speaking nations.

The Groundwork of Ideology in the
Rejection of Pure Reason

Kant's philosophy was the bridge between the Enlightenment, which held that science and reason could solve every human problem, and Romanticism, in which an entirely different basis was sought for morality, religion and even philosophy itself (1:40). Without being an ideologist himself in a strict sense, Kant laid the intellectual groundwork for ideology through his radical departure from Rationalism, which made no sharp distinction between the laws of nature and normative principles. This departure is focused in the basic question of Kant's *Critique of Pure Reason* which is, "how are *a priori* synthetic judgments possible?" (40:50, 70, 80; 42: 26, 29). His answer to this is based on the premise that we can no longer think of our understanding as a passive mirror which reflects intuitively the patterns of things in themselves; it is an active agency which orders the raw material of sensory experience into a conceptualized and systematized world of phenomena.

Kant effected his revolution in philosophy by showing that the usual categories of thought such as "cause" and "substance" do not represent actual entities or real relations; they are not inherent in the nature of things but are procedural ideas and rules which must be accepted pragmatically as conceptual tools for the purpose of controlling the world. He realized that the standards of rationality are not "written into the heavens but are adopted by active beings as practical necessities" (1:58,61). Even though he rejected all claims of metaphysical knowledge of reality, he did accept certain convictions as postulates which were necessary to give meaning and coherence to human experience; for example, his postulates of the pure practical reason did not give knowledge in a theoretical sense but rather served as practical imperatives which guide men in the process of human decision. Kant rejected pure theoretical reason and held that the only legitimate metaphysical convictions

26

are those which are based upon the needs and demands of the moral will. On the basis of his distinction of the "two reasons" he removed the domain of moral philosophy completely out of the realm of the scientific method, since its foundations lie in the will rather than in the intellect alone; but even though ethics is not purely theoretical, it is still a "rational" discipline. By the fact that Kant elevated practical reason (moral will) above scientific under-standing, he effected the shift where philosophy removes itself from the status of a super-science to a status approaching ideology (1: 38). Nevertheless, even though Kant laid much of the conceptual groundwork for the ideology which was developed by Fichte and Hegel, it is highly unlikely that he would have identified himself with ideology because of his strong tendency to euphemize the 'moral will' by referring to it as a form of strictly rational activity.

The Origin of 'Ideology' and
Its Various Usages

Destutt de Tracy and the Origin of 'Ideology'.—The origin of the word 'ideology' is traceable to the French philosopher Destutt de Tracy (1754-1836), who introduced it in 1796 as a philosophical, epistemological, and anthropological term to be used in connection with his radically empirical analysis of the human mind (Ap. 42). It is difficult to say exactly what he meant by the term, but Naess seems to think a good approximation of a definition would be the "general doctrine about ideas," taking "ideas" in the sense used by Locke and Condillac. Naess thinks that the term was not intended as a name for particular doctrines about ideas, for example, those of Destutt de Tracy, but as a term designating the particular meth-ods and approaches which Destutt de Tracy represented within philosophy, pedagogics, and the other humanistic disciplines. This usage accounts for the fact that Destutt de Tracy and his followers were called "the ideologists" by the public in general as well as by themselves (72:149).

According to Destutt de Tracy, 'ideology,' along with grammar and logic, is a part of 'zoology.' He did not strictly define 'zoology,' but his inclusion of ideology in it suggests that he considered ideas to have a close relation to the natural sciences. This conclusion is supported by the fact that his approach is (unadmittedly meta-physically) naturalistic, in contradistinction to the metaphysical, theological, and authoritarian approaches that he opposed. It was at this point that his approach resembles that of Condillac (72: 150).

Ideological Ideas Used as Weapons.—It is significant that, along with Destutt de Tracy, the leaders of the French Revolution used their claim that "sensation is the origin of all ideas" as a weapon and tool to break down all forms of authority opposed to their own aims. During this Revolutionary period, Napoleon found himself on the same side as the French ideologists. When the Revolutionary government gained power, it recognized this materialism as the only philosophy and the ideologues, as they later came to be known, as the only true philosophers.

The Negative Usage of 'Ideology' in the Napoleonic Era.—In the Napoleonic era 'ideology' gained a new shade of meaning through the influence of Napoleon and Chateaubriand. When Napoleon gained a position of absolute authority, he became the target of the ideologists who now became his opponents; this led him to refer to both 'ideologues' and 'ideology' in a contemptuous manner. Naess thinks that at the time no cognitive meaning was given to the latter term: outside the circle of Destutt de Tracy's influence, it came to connote among the pro-Bonapartist public something low and unrespectable. This derogatory meaning has persisted even though it is neither original nor etymologically accurate; Roucek speaks of a "popular connotation of the term as visionary moonshine" (87:482), and Webster lists as one significa-tion, "visionary speculation, idle theorizing, also, an impractical theory or system of theories."

Bonald's Neutral Usage of 'Ideology'.—As early as 1800, another French philosopher, Bonald, employed the terms 'ideologie' and 'ideologique,' apparently without knowing about Destutt de Tracy's use of the word. On the subject of ideology, Bonald strongly opposed both the philosophers whom Destutt de Tracy favored and the philosophies in general which were based upon analysis of ideas (in the Lockian sense) and language. As a political op-ponent of the French Revolution and therefore of Destutt de Tracy and his friends, Bonald had respect for the church and defended it from the attacks of the materialists, emphatically criticizing what he called "ideologie (moderne) ." Naess suggests Bonald used the terms as broadly or loosely synonymous with "la science de l'esprit human" (72:152) , that is, to name a branch of knowledge. The connotations given by Bonald to 'ideology' are somewhat similar to some of those it had for Destutt de Tracy; the difference between these two men was essentially one of attitude. Where Destutt de Tracy gave a positive estimation to the contents of the various treatises on ideology of his day, Bonald in direct opposition showed a form of negative appreciation; it is possible that Napoleon's negative use of the word came in part from this source.

As used in the early 19th century, the term 'ideology' was obviously ambiguous. Naess distinguishes two distinct meanings of the term, which he denominates *Ideology I* and *Ideology II*. The first suggests the meaning of the "total mass of ideas of mankind or of another zoological species." The second refers to the "general doctrine about the total mass of ideas of mankind or of another zoological species."

The Emotional and Volitional Usages of 'Ideology'.—Along with these two possible connotations of the world 'ideology,' Naess detects in Destutt de Tracy's work indications of liberalism, anticlericalism, and naturalistic, scientific reductionism. Destutt de Tracy used such an approach as this to justify his own ideas and plans of action both in education and politics. Meanwhile, during the period of Napoleon's power 'ideology' gained a third shade of meaning, to which Naess refers as *Ideology III* (72:152) . As a consequence of Napoleon's campaign against the ideologists, the words 'ideology' and 'ideologists' now acquired very strong emotional and volitional elements of meaning which were derogatory to Destutt de Tracy and his followers. Later this third sense of the term became that which was most widely used, making it much more hazy and non-cognitive. Marx was one who used the term in such a sense.

Marx's Emotional and Negative Use of 'Ideology'.—Shortly after 1840, Marx began to use the term 'ideology.' At this time it had some vogue in print among writers who were at once careless and influential, as a term connoting heat rather than light (72:153) . Contrary to Destutt de Tracy, who usually meant by 'ideology' the mass of human ideas and the general science of ideas, Marx was inclined to use it to denote a particular class of normative opinion which generally related to moral, theological, metaphysical, and political subjects. For Destutt de Tracy an idea is epistemologically neutral; Marx tended to contrast it with truth and knowledge (72:157). Marx's most frequent use of the term 'ideology' was in *Die Deutsche Ideologie,* a work that was extremely argumentative and polemical and lacked a purpose to be scientific in the fashion of *Das Kapital* (72:154). In it he uses the term 'ideologie' about fifty times but without any normative, descriptive, or real definition of it. In fact, his loose usage makes it difficult to determine what he specifically meant by it. Naess thinks that Marx's intention in using the word was comparatively "shallow" and that there is no reason to believe that he wanted to make 'ideology' one of his key concepts, since it held no central position in his terminology.

Marx's Alleged Distinction between Ideology and "Real Knowledge."—Light may be shed on Marx's use of 'ideology' by considering how he compared it to "real knowledge." In *Die Deutsche Ideologie,* particularly, Marx seems to be making an effort to distinguish between the "ideological" factors of consciousness in contradistinction to "real knowledge" and "real positive science." Unfortunately he did not make the distinction perfectly clear; although he did hint that ideologies, and the reasons why people accept them, are non-rational. These ideologies appear among his opponents in the form of theories of knowledge, metaphysics, ethics, religion, and all other forms of consciousness which tend to reveal the basic attitudes or commitments of a definite social class. For the most part Marx was inclined not to use the term 'idea' in connection with his own doctrines, preferring to refer to them as "positive science," which was in his estimation a description of reality (72:156).

Marx's Merger of Theory and Practice.—Marx's vigorous criticism of other ideologies was based upon his belief that they had wrongly given pure theory a position which was too exalted. Although he could not avoid the use of abstractions, he acknowledged that they were only a convenient means of classifying and ordering the account of the processes of history. Marx, in his approach to the basis of "positive science," claimed that by realizing that theory has no independent function he was able to avoid the mistakes of his enemies; pure theory in the sense it was used by Kant and Hegel has no "real existence." The realness of a theory, on the contrary, consists in its relation to actions which are useful in changing the environment (66:199); the criterion for a good theory is purely pragmatic. Truth which has no relation to action is a reversion to scholastic nonsense; communism is not a system of ideas or pure theory of an ideal; it is rather "reality" that produces the ideas. Marx regarded his own descriptions of communism as ideas, doctrines, and opinions in much the same sense that descriptions within empirical science might be regarded as ideas, doctrines, and opinions (72:156, 157)

It is difficult to know the exact relationship Marx held to exist between ideology and science or knowledge; neither he nor his followers have ever given an adequate account of this relation. At any rate, it is manifest that Marx generally associated ideology with both irrationality and ulterior social or political motives and goals. Since these motives were not scientifically based on "fact," Marx regarded the theories that resulted from these ideas as merely the superstructure of culture. Thus, any such ideological ideas would be without cognitive content and could have no autonomous development within the process of history (1:17, 18).

Since Marx and his pre-Leninist followers have generally used the term 'ideology' and its derivatives for the purpose of polemics, its adoption in subsequent Western thought has thereby been considerably influenced against any neutral use of the word. It is generally held that Marx used 'ideology' with the significance given to it by Napoleon and Chateaubriand, not with that which it had for Destutt de Tracy. Destutt de Tracy did not use the word to imply "visionary moonshine." This meaning was first introduced by Napoleon when he sought to discredit the ideologues. Although the notion that Marx's use of the word paralleled that of Napoleon must be taken only as a rough approximation (72:153, 154), what is at any rate clear is that the former considered ideology to be inferior to "positive science" even after it had become highly developed through the philosophically formidable systems of Fichte and Hegel.

The Neutral Role of 'Ideology'.—On the other hand Marx sometimes used the word 'idea' and its derivatives in a manner similar to its employment in the writings of Locke, Condillac, and Destutt de Tracy. Perhaps Naess is right in his suggestion that Marx's use of 'ideology' at times was an expansion of 'idea' as it is used by these writers to mean something like a "systematic development and an explicitly integrated comprehensive group of opinions" (72:155). In this usage the concept would be fairly neutral and would contrast with the pejorative way he employs it on many occasions. It was not beyond Marx and particularly his followers to have the conception that ideology could have its own type of validity if thought of in the proper relation of being subordinate to his materialistic concept of history. Thus, he does have some place for a neutral use of the term 'ideology,' that is, neutral according to his own materialistic metaphysics. Some of Marx's followers in the 19th century used 'ideology' in a nondepreciatory fashion. Lassalle (49:115) in his speech in Frankfurt a. M., May, 1863, considered himself to be an ideologist with highly praiseworthy goals (72:159). Engels spoke of "a clear ideology" as "the deduction of a reality not from the reality itself, but from imagination." He also said, "The real driving force which moves it [ideology] remains unconscious, otherwise it would not be an ideological process" (87:482).

Marx's Inconsistency Concerning 'Ideology'.—In his use of 'ideology' Marx was inconsistent, chiefly because he employed the term for polemic rather than for honest scientific analysis; his main purpose in using the word was to ridicule certain German doctrines in the fields of metaphysics, epistemology, and value that claimed, as "pure" theories, to have a validity apart from his materialistic brand of "positive science." Marx regarded these theoretical approaches as social myths or opiates of the people, and he thought that the "reasons" which actually led people to accept these doctrines were ulterior motives which had nothing to do with concrete facts or logic. Unfortunately this arbitrary concept of ideology has continued until the present time (1:19). Nevertheless, there has been a new revitalization of the positive connotations of 'ideology' in contemporary thought. This positive use, in fact, has not been totally without the help of Marx's followers.

32

The Use of 'Ideology' in Contemporary Marxist-Leninist Circles

In contemporary Marxist-Leninist circles, in contradistinction to the period before Lenin, there has been a decided change in the use of the word 'ideology,' which no longer refers only to the enemies of Marxism-Leninism but now also to the Marxist-Leninists themselves. *The Program of the Communist International,* for example, speaks of "Means of Ideological Influence" (Ap. 43); and Khrushchev himself has said, "ideology is our strongest weapon" (Ap. 44). The evidence will subsequently be considered and amplified in chapter 3 that the Marxist-Leninists now use 'ideology' eulogistically, in connection with the primary definition implied earlier in this chapter with reference to the use of ideas as tools and weapons.

The Present Status of 'Ideology' in Contemporary Western Intellectual Circles

Even though in former times Marx and early Marxists were mainly responsible for confusing the use of the word 'ideology,' since Lenin this confusion has been preserved by the non-Marxist-Leninists in general and by Western sociologists in particular. In contemporary literature there is a considerable variety of definitions of 'ideology,' although many of them are rather arbitrary and etymologically inaccurate, as is the case of that offered by Karl Mannheim in his influential *Ideology and Utopia* (62:177).

A rather complete treatment of the various definitions of 'ideology' today is that given by Arne Naess (72:16ff), who treats in detail of their various nuances. Naess maintains that the word 'ideology' through its short history has had such a wide variety of definitions among social scientists and writers in general that there is very little reason to expect any uniformity in the employment of this term. He suggests that as a result of current popular usage it has assumed importance more from a causal than from a cognitive point of view (72:144, 147); usually reference to 'ideology' signifies the use of doctrine to affect the attitude of the hearer rather than to inform with clear meaning. In extreme cases ideological language may have practically no cognitive meaning at all, and is employed not to clarify the mind but to stir the will to action. Naess thinks that the present status of objectivity in technical literature dealing with ideology is very low compared with sciences such as physics and geology (72:226), since very few influential thinkers have made any attempt to develop ideology research at a reasonably high level of objectivity.

The variety of contemporary definitions of the word 'ideology' usually ranges somewhere between the two given by Oxford's *New English Dictionary*:

1. The science of ideas; that department of philosophy or psychology which deals with the origin and nature of ideas. b. spec. Applied to the system of the French philosopher Condillac, according to which all ideas are derived from sensations. (Ap. 45)
2. Ideal or abstract speculation; in a depreciatory sense, unpractical or visionary theorizing or speculation. (101:20)

It would serve no important purpose to treat this great spectrum of opinion since the purpose of this inquiry is to distill only the essential characteristics of the most developed ideologies.

Aiken, however, shares neither Naess's pessimism nor Mannheim's confusion in his efforts to bring order into the subject of ideology research. His method, similar to my own, is to distill essential characteristics of the most highly developed ideological philosophies, rather than to try to find something common in every system that goes under the name of ideology. He is one of the few writers on the subject who has made philosophical sense out of the tendency of ideologists to rely heavily upon subjective factors. Aiken shows that the differences between the subjective factors of well developed ideology and those of traditional philosophy are essentially matters of degree rather than kind, since traditional philosophy has merely called such factors by other names. For example, much of what has been considered *a priori* or intuitively rational has turned out to be merely a strong belief. These elements of passion and action tend to force subjective beliefs into focus as an important factor; but it is not merely the ideologies that do this. Aiken says,

> Every philosophical picture of reality . . . presupposes a
> way of thinking about it, a rule or principle of conceptual
> organization which must simply be accepted by its maker. Thus
> the element of subjectivity, however subtly disguised, can
> never be wholly eliminated from any philosophical system.
> Every such system, consciously or otherwise, presupposes cer-
> tain ultimate commitments or "posits." These are made by the
> rational animal himself in order that he may live and do his
> work, and their validity has no higher court of appeal than
> his own determination to abide by them. (1:15)

As Aiken's statement suggests, every philosophical system must have
certain presuppositions. The ideologies, upon closer examination,
are not seriously different from the traditional philosophies in the
choosing of their basic premises, although ideologies in general
have not exercised the intellectual rigor common to traditional
philosophies. This does not mean that none of them has been
philosophically respectable. Aiken has pointed out that the works
of a number of the great 19th century thinkers may be classified
as both ideology and good philosophy.

Even though ideologies have generally included a considerable
element of belief or subjective factors, many of which were not too
well grounded, this does not necessarily imply that all ideologies
are irrational. The word 'ideology' itself does not necessarily imply
irrationality even though there have been a substantial number
of irrational ideologies (87:480). This holds true in the same
fashion that the word 'philosophy' does not necessarily imply a
naturalistic leaning just because there have been a great number
of naturalistically oriented philosophies. Aiken explains this by
his own analysis of the meaning of the term:

> My use of the term "ideology" is quite neutral in these re-
> spects. No doubt, the ideological commitments of the nine-
> teenth-century philosophers can be contrasted with factual
> beliefs of the sort entertained by men of common sense or by
> men of science in their capacity as scientists. But this does not
> in the least imply that they are irrational or that they are
> proposed or accepted without reason. Hegel provides a case in
> point. He did not for a moment suppose that his philosophy
> of history belongs to positive science. But he did formulate
> it in a highly critical and self-conscious way, and he offers what

35

Mill called "considerations to influence the intellect" which, in his judgement, should render it plausible and perhaps acceptable to any disinterested person. Moreover, even if most of the philosophical theses of the nineteenth-century philosophers are properly called "ideological," in contrast to the theories of empirical science, this by no means implies that there are no important relations, save those of contrast and/or opposition, between them. (1:19)

It is in such an observation as Aiken's that it becomes evident that the new emphasis in metaphysics (which stressed the basic commitments involved in being a civilized, rational, human being) has been essentially practical rather than theoretical (Ap. 46). This consuming concern for the practical and the conduct of life gave rise to the strongly ideological philosophies (1:ix). These new systems of ideas were a contrast to the traditional philosophies of Greece and Scholasticism in that ideas were no longer ontologically limited to some eternal realm or universal status to be considered in purely theoretical fashion, but became methodological tools by which men's beliefs, intentions and plans were implemented and fortified.

The most developed forms of contemporary ideology continue in accord with the historical ideologies treated by Aiken. The remainder of this inquiry will be a treatment of contemporary ideology in both its morally destructive (chapter 3) and its morally creative forms.

MARXIST-LENINIST IDEOLOGY
AND MORALITY

An adequate understanding of Marxist-Leninist ideology and morality requires a consideration of (a) its foundations, (b) its instrumental expressions, internal and external, and (c) its human goals.

The Foundations of Marxist-Leninist Morality

Marx himself had no systematic ethical theory; consequently his ethical principles must be deduced from his writings generally and chiefly from the moral evaluations he made of social institutions. On the basis of these evaluations he proceeded to give form to his ideology (if not to a strict moral philosophy) (Ap. 47) which became the historical foundations for later Marxist-Leninists; from these, in turn, evolved two basic principles of Marxist-Leninist morality, for example, their normative foundations and volitional foundations.

Historical Foundations.—The essential nature of Marxist-Leninist morality is most effectively grasped by examining its historical philosophical foundations, which are derivatives of its ultimate aims (Ap. 48) of social and political revolution. Marx's condemnation of the capitalistic system is essentially a moral one, and roots in his repudiation of its identification of labor power with a commodity. To him capitalism has made slaves of the working class because it has caused men to sell themselves on the market. Consequently, his final aim was to abolish all private property and hence the capitalistic system. Since the *a priori* foundation of his morality was an eschatological aim, moral acts are those which fulfill this aim. Thus the key to the understanding of Marxist-Leninist morality is that morality itself is a tool of ideology rather than its judge.

Marx has given modern communism its basic doctrinal foundation, but an examination of this alone is not sufficient to give us full understanding of its contemporary morality. Just as a major part of its theory came from Germany, so a considerable part of its practical approach has its roots in the history of Russian socialism. The Russian socialist movement, a form of left wing Hegelianism, was championed by a number of men, like Belinsky, in the 1840's. This philosophy expressed itself in a break with abstract idealism and in a materialistic emphasis upon actual concrete fact. Belinsky had great sympathy with mankind, but still at the same time he was willing to preach brutality and tyranny. In his mind there was no way to avoid bloodshed; and he held that, if necessary, to cut off the heads of hundreds of thousands was a justifiable way to bring happiness to the major part of mankind. Belinsky claimed that people are so stupid that they must be dragged to happiness by force (5:41).

During the 1860's, Russian materialism developed into a position very different from its Western form; it turned into a brand of dogmatic theology, with its own dogma of moral obligation. Underlying these factors was a hidden distinctive nihilist asceticism (5:46). The main historical streams from Marx and the Russian socialists, however, found their most effective merger in the life and ideology of Lenin, who had worked out a systematic philosophy of instrumental values to be carried out in the practical order of action in revolutionary conflict.

Lenin fought for a consistency and wholeness in the conflict that was possible only on the basis on his dogmatic outlook, which was really an orthodoxy based on a confession of faith in a totalitarian system that would not allow a single element to be removed. His philosophy of moral action was Machiavellian, sanctioning the use of any method effective in the fight to achieve revolution. The 'good' was now identified with everything which aided the revolution; whatever hindered this was 'evil' (49:536). Even though his principles were morally derived from his dislike of injustice, exploitation, and oppression, his totalistic revolutionary idea made him insensitive to the evil in his own methods. Lenin was systematic in his subordination of individual issues to the social whole and in elaborating the tactical (Ap. 49) problem of acquiring and

38

maintaining political power (49:538; 93:1048). In 1920, he made the claim that "our morality is entirely subordinated to the interest of the class struggle of the proletariat" (49:536). This spirit is still present in current Soviet morality (Ap. 50).

Normative Foundations.—In referring to the 'normative' foundations of Marxism-Leninism, it is necessary to bear in mind that in this system norms have a different function from that accepted in the non-communist democracies. Whereas the democracies are inclined to use moral norms to judge ideology, communist ideology, on the contrary, (through its claim of being the very basis of science) judges morality and allows itself to be judged by nothing. In communist morality norms are basically conceptual tools which are used to accomplish a predetermined task. For this reason, as Northrop has pointed out, Marxism-Leninism and the Western democracies have wholly different approaches to moral norms; hence questions of international law are unable to find common ground of discussion (Ap. 51).

Even though the communist normative scheme is essentially instrumental, it does embody a definite sense of values. Official communist literature contains an abundance of highly charged value terms, which seem ambiguous in connection with their materialism until one realizes the dominant role played by their ideology. If there is any one main normative foundation for Marxian moral ideals, this is the overall Marxist-Leninist strategy (84: 264, 265) (Ap. 49), which in ideological terms is called a historical "fact." It is on this "factual" basis that the communists assert that with their aim of strategy there can be no compromise and that its pursuit must be constant and undeviating. Current news events show the obvious lack of agreement among the Russian and Chinese Marxists, and these show a marked difference from the more nationalistic varieties of the smaller nations of Eastern Europe, etc. Nevertheless, my argument still holds for the traditional revolutionary Marxism-Leninism, which is the normative root and basic theme of all these later variations. When this ceases to be the case, these later modifications will be something other than Marxism-Leninism.

The Marxists also accept a scale of instrumental values, the highest among which is the international dictatorship of the proletariat.

It is this privileged instrumental value which orders subordinate values in a manner to make them most effective according to the needs of the time. This instrumental use of moral ideals, which may seem inconsistent to the outsider, is really a highly developed form of ideological tactics. We must understand the difference between Marxist-Leninist strategy and tactics if we are to comprehend their scale of values at any given time and situation in history. Communist strategy remains relatively constant; tactics change often, even to the point of apparent compromise (75:256).

Volitional Foundations.—The volitional foundations of Marxist-Leninist morality are rooted in ideology, even if they cannot be found in the explicit doctrine. This is consonant with the fact that communist ideology has usually found a way to revitalize recalcitrant doctrine. It also helps to resolve the apparent paradox that a deterministic position is in practice able to appeal to voluntary decision and action.

Lenin was too clever an ideologist to be shackled by a strict determinism. Although he continued to pay lip service to the doctrine of historical determinism, he introduced elements of freedom, choice, and creativity into both individual and historical action, and even insisted upon the importance of the striving human will when this was the will of a dedicated and disciplined revolutionary (45:571).

According to some modern Soviet writers, Lenin's innovation is really a modification of determinism; among them P. A. Shariya called such a variation "relative freedom of choice" (45:571). Contemporary Russian thinkers recognize and accept the fact of an evolution of dogma in their own official philosophy (9:64), which V. G. Baskakov refers to as "creative development" (Ap. 52).

By its very definition, according to this point of view, revolutionary freedom must be free to bring change. Since the overall aim of Marxism is revolution, any ideological concept of freedom must be revolutionary or change-causing. Berdyaev has noted the difference between the original Marxist doctrine and the ideological approach of contemporary Marxist-Leninists; consequently, in spite of the alleged determinism and materialism of basic communist philosophical doctrines, he is able to detect the ideological importance of freedom in contemporary Russian thought. With penetrating insight into the ideological approach to freedom, Berdyaev has shown that the communists have a very different notion of freedom from that traditional in the West (Ap. 53). The Marxian revolutionary thinks that freedom is not a liberty for the individual to go to the right or left; rather it is freedom for the social man to be undivided in his energies to move totally, under the dictatorship of the proletariat, in the direction of a new society. Real freedom, in other words, is freedom to change life, to re-make men and the world. The personal freedom of the revolutionary is elective, the embodiment of an ability and a responsibility to join and foster the revolutionary movement. This is not, however, a freedom of thought and conscience; it is the elective opportunity to accept and hasten the coming of the new age through the "purity" of a supra-personal purpose. It is here that the Marxist becomes a very close counterfeit of Christianity.

Internal Instrumental Expressions
of Marxist-Leninist Morality

Regarded from the standpoint of its particular moral expressions as a means of advancing communism within communist-dominated nations, the instrumental expression of Marxist-Leninist morality may be divided into two basic categories: the one concerns the use of moral ideas as tools and weapons of the class struggle within communist societies like Soviet Russia (45:571); the other concerns the use of "moral" ideas as ideological weapons against the enemies of Marxism (Ap. 54). In specific character these two embodiments of revolutionary purpose differ considerably; but their underlying principles are identical; in whatever form or expression the Marxist-Leninists use moral ideas, they are always essentially "instruments through which class warfare is carried on" (27:143).

These various facets of the Marxist-Leninist ideological thrust reveal certain important aspects of ideology that the traditional analytic approach does not exhaust. Since ideology is so intimately bound up with the facts of will and belief, it has to be treated in an empirical manner that cannot be handled effectively by mere conceptual analysis of 'good,' 'right,' and the like. In considering ideology, it is necessary to adopt the spirit of Ockham and proceed

41

from the particular to the general, because there are very few impartial ready-made general concepts about ideology. What general concepts are available are mostly false and inadequate. Consequently, since I am concerned here to show the relationship between Marxist-Leninist ideology and morality, this ideology will be examined in terms of its particular, concrete moral expressions, which are, in this system, of an instrumental nature. Only on this basis is it possible to escape the muddle that has surrounded one of the most dynamic facts of contemporary history.

Let us begin our examination of some of the Marxist-Leninist virtues in their extensive development as ideological weapons within their social system. These virtues are: (a) clarity of purpose, (b) responsibility, (c) purity, (d) unity, (e) totality, (f) self-criticism, (g) change, and (h) ideals.

Clarity of Purpose.—The Marxist-Leninists realize that clarity of purpose is absolutely basic and indispensable to ideology, because without this virtue none of the other virtues can rise to the full level of ideological effectiveness. This explains why clarity of purpose was stressed at the Party Congress of 1960 as an ideological duty for every worker (86:744), and it was stressed that it is an ideological "ought" for everyone in labor to be clear of purpose so that he can make his machine, tractor, lathe, or other tools work most effectively for "lofty" goals.

Responsibility.—Responsibility is one of the first progeny of clarity of purpose, and it seems to be one that the Marxists have established widely and in an effective manner. Under party discipline and control an unbroken chain of responsibility can be traced, at least theoretically speaking, from the worker to the nation, from lowest to highest echelons. In this respect, the Marxist-Leninists have the advantage over the Western democracies; in Russia the category of responsibility is well established prior to the ideological notion of instrumental freedom, and on this basis it is much easier to go from moral cooperation and order toward its individualistic exceptions than it is to reverse the process. If, as in the democracies, we posit freedom first, then the human psyche tends to leave little from which to create a wholistic sense of responsibility (Ap. 55).

In the Twenty-First Party Congress, the decision was made

that, "together with the other Communist Parties, the C. P. S. U. [bears] responsibility for the destinies of the Socialist camp, the destinies of the world Communist movement" (86:739, 36:35). Translated from ideological to ordinary language, this means that the Soviets accept as their responsibility the mission to turn the whole world (Ap. 56) into a communist society as the only right fulfillment of its "destiny." The principle of responsibility, as understood by the Marxists, gains force from the emotive value of the word "destiny" and from the inherent *dynamic* of eschatological totalism; this completeness of scope generates in the revolutionary its own kind of mental "freedom," i.e. liberation from demands for rights and disputes concerning their legitimate limits. It is only on the basis of this extensive attitude of responsibility that purity obtains an adequate volitional foundation to become actual, rather than to remain a mere intellectual ideal.

Purity.—The Marxist-Leninists frequently state the absolute indispensability of ideological purity (Ap. 57), an extensive term that roughly corresponds to the Western philosophical concept of consistency. The Twenty-First Party Congress passed a resolution using the concept 'purity' which states that the C.P.S.U. would continue

> . . . "to follow faithfully the great international teaching of Marx, Engels, and Lenin, combat revisionists of all hues, uphold the purity of Marxism-Leninism, and work for new successes of the world Communist and working-class movement." (86:739)

'Purity' is a word frequently used in the *History of the C.P.S.U.*, often in stressing the duty of an "uncompromising struggle for the purity of Marxist-Leninist theory . . . " (86:749, 727).

The fact that the Soviets use the word 'purity' in connection with 'theory' does not in the least degree weaken its moral or obligational status. Since in Marxism-Leninism theory is inseparably bound to practice (Ap. 58), the linking of the concept of 'purity' with 'theory' in no way gives it moral neutrality. In its total scope the Marxist-Leninist idea of purity, taken as a definite moral category, also contains a strong religious undercurrent (Ap. 59); in many ways it is very similar to the Christian idea of purity of heart.

The Marxist-Leninists know that singleness of purpose, in heart and mind, i.e. purity, is an absolute moral necessity for revolutionary ideology. In this point Russian doctrine has given emphasis to a dynamic moral category that has not been satisfactorily recognized and treated in conventional Western philosophy. On the one hand, philosophy has tended to identify effective motives for right action with grasped intellectual concepts, particularly that of enlightened self-interest; on the other hand, academic moral thinking has tended recently to omit the problem of the dynamics of action and to concentrate on the theoretical question of the nature of moral categories. This has strongly tended to submerge the motivation problem and to stress the logical principle of consistency within a system of clear and distinct theoretical ideas. It is assumed that effective action and commitment will take care of themselves. Marxist-Leninist thought is here more perceptive; it recognizes in 'purity' a moral principle of preeminent importance, and one not to be preempted by logical consistency. 'Purity' is here identified with ideology, analogous to the Christian principle of purity of heart which cannot be understood apart from a grasp of the nature of decisional faith as linked to knowledge. I wish to make the point that it is in such moral categories as ideological purity that we may find the data which give insight into the dynamic moralities of the world. Instrumental moralities like that of Marxism-Leninism seemingly have more motivational *dynamic* than traditional philosophical ethics. So far as this is the case it is an exceedingly consequential fact. Why it is the case will be considered later.

Unity.—The Marxist-Leninist concept of 'unity' is an essential cog in their moral machinery. The 1960 *History of the C.P.S.U.,* in dealing with "Unity of the Communist Party," makes it emphatic that the universal establishment of communism will succeed

> only if the internal life of the Party is highly *organized,* if all its organizations and all its members have *one* will, if they act as a *solid* force, if there is *iron discipline* in its ranks. (86:755, 756)

This solidarity is, of course, a moral and political unity based on the ideology of Marxism-Leninism (86:760). It is also a moral category deduced from Marxist-Leninist ideology. The words they have italicized suggest this very strongly and indicate the major role played by will in harmony with Marxist-Leninist theory as well as one will in harmony with other human wills. This working combination of will and theory gives revolutionary instrumental morality its ideological effectiveness.

Totality.—Since Marxism-Leninism is a class revolution and its morality is an instrument of ideology, it has developed a totalistic approach that is exceeded only by the higher expressions of Christianity. 'Totalism' means essentially a total dedication to a world revolution; it comprehends a totality in scope (internationalism) as the end, and totality of means to obtain this end. Totality in scope signifies the universal spread of communism and the consequent destruction of competing social-economic systems, whether capitalist or non-Marxist forms of socialism:

> By upholding the principle of proletarian internationalism, the C.P.S.U. has discharged, and continues to discharge, its duty to the international proletariat. The programme, strategy and tactics of the Leninist Party, and its entire practical activity, are permeated with the spirit of proletarian internationalism. (86:759, 760)

Such totalism is a cult of complete destruction of competitors; it repudiates good will towards heresies, and it is an ideological concept in which all things, including individual men, are mere tools of revolution.

In this totalistic view there are virtually no social factors outside of the active domain of the Marxist-Leninist revolutionary, which is best exemplified by his ability to twist the unconscious and subconscious propensities of even his enemies toward their own destruction. The revolution includes all classes and types, one way or another, in which the victim(s) may either cooperate or be eliminated from the path of the revolution by various means. (The only thing that Marxist-Leninists have found they cannot use to their advantage in any way is a man or group that possesses a morally superior ideology which goes beyond class [Ap. 60].)

With respect to the use of human factors, used in the form of both conscious and unconscious cooperation, totalism regards the use of every effective possibility as a necessary obligation, necessary if their ideological strategy is to be fully revolutionary. The revolutionary man "must focus this world into one invincible destructive force" (5:64). He is under moral obligation to use every possible force to the advantage of the revolution, even the good will and peace efforts of his enemies. In 1931, Dimitri Manuilsky, of the Lenin School of Political Warfare, suggested that the totalism of Marxist-Leninist tactics included the use of "peace" as an ideological tool of destruction:

> War to the hilt between Communism and Capitalism is inevitable. Today, of course, we are not strong enough to attack. Our time will come in twenty to thirty years. The bourgeoisie will have to be put to sleep, so we will begin by launching the most spectacular peace movement on record. There will be electrifying overtures and unheard-of-concessions. The capitalist countries, stupid and decadent, will rejoice to cooperate in their own destruction. They will leap at another chance to be friends. As soon as their guard is down we shall smash them with our clenched fist . . . (69:22)

The Marxist-Leninist virtue of totalism, in sum, is a totalism of obligation to develop an ideological usage for every force in the world (5:64), whether physical or mental, good or evil, noble or base, materialistic or spiritual.

Self-Criticism.—One of the fundamental norms of Marxist-Leninist morality that gives surprise to the democratic Westerner is the concept of 'the obligation of self-criticism.' This cardinal principle, which can be traced to Marx, has been employed with considerable success in Russia. In the words of the party history,

> The history of the C.P.S.U. teaches us that *bold* criticism of its own shortcomings, weaknesses and mistakes is a major condition for the successes of a party. The activity of the C.P.S.U. provides brilliant confirmation of Marx's idea that constant criticism and self-criticism are a distinctive feature of the proletarian revolution, that they constitute a law of its development. (86:757)

Self-criticism, however, is not directed to the ultimate strategy of the proletarian revolution; it is limited to whatever hinders tactical success (Ap. 61). This principle of self-criticism toward the hindrances of the revolution was invoked in a spectacular way by Khrushchev in his attack on Stalinism. Contemporary Russian Marxist-Leninists, however, propose to hold to a mean position between "revisionism," on one side, and "dogmatism," on the other.

Creativity.—Closely associated with self-criticism is the concept of 'creativity' (Ap. 62). One of the roles of self-criticism is to cultivate the "creativity" of all citizens to bring about a revolutionary transformation of society (86:756; 9:10). As has been previously noted, this has many expressions and a great breadth of scope. Ideological morality has its own type of creativity which can only come from a somewhat realistic form of self-criticism. The counterpart of this self-criticism in Christian morality is humility, the ground of its creativity.

Change.—Another factor, linked with operational tactics, and one that underlies it, is that of fluidity or change, which serves realistically as a mediating principle between instrumental purposes and their highly idealized expectations of history, society, and man. As purely utopian and doctrinaire, undisciplined by hardheaded realism, the revolutionary movement would have collapsed from dreamy idealism; recognition of change as intrinsic to the actual scene of history permits practical readjustments to the unforeseen and unpredictable shifting of classes (91:105, 112) in a fluid world. The theory of Marxism, including basic strategy, remains fixed; but on other levels the principle "enables the Party to ascertain the laws governing social life, to find the right orientation in any situation . . . " (86:748). The revolutionary is taught and learns to change himself so as to make the best out of every situation and circumstance in order to bring communism. This includes, of course, the important shift of orientation: change from self-interest to social interest is a fixed principle of the system and must be continually increased in completeness.

Ideals.—Because of its materialistic naturalism, the writings of Marx have given historians and commentators the notion that the categories of ideology and the spiritual were unworthy of a true Marxist (27:141). However, this is not the case in Marxism-Leninism, which has moved ideology from its implicit to its explicitly exhalted place. In subsequent Russian communism, particularly of late, these spiritual categories have been made explicit.

The quasi-idealistic inclination to identify speculative or scientific hypothesis and moral dogma is indigenous to the Russian tradition which, as Berdyaev has noted, tends in turn to be linked with worship; and this has been manifest among Russian revolutionaries (5:21). It began with the radical intelligentsia who treated Western evolutionary ideas as a religious type of dogma, like revelation. What Western scientific thinkers regarded as hypothesis became an object of fervid devotion among many of the intellectual leaders; to many of them, for example, Darwinism was an object of devotion, and scepticism regarding it was regarded as a moral deviation. The early revolutionaries invariably exalted some relative or contingent idea into an absolute and then made it an object of spiritual devotion (5:21). They have, to this day, spiritualized their beliefs about natural and social science into an absolutistic and scientistic dogma demanding total moral response (Ap. 63).

In spite of the scientistic character of their system, contemporary Marxist-Leninists have not forsaken a type of idealism that explicitly calls for action that will lead to a genuine flowering of "spiritual good of humanity" (36:129). Such "spirituality" of philosophical materialists is incomprehensible unless we take into account that their materialistic philosophy is itself the offspring of ideology, and bear in mind that all well developed ideologies, whatever their philosophical dogmas, have a spiritual or quasi-religious component. Ideology will continue unless science finds a means of reducing elements like will, commitment and faith into purely descriptive categories (Ap. 64). This is, however, highly improbable. It is therefore imperative to study the self-chosen "spirituality" of Marxist-Leninists in order to understand them ideologically, as well as to grasp their more superficial philosophical side.

External Instrumental Expressions of Marxist-Leninist Morality

Ordinary moral philosophies have traditionally centered themselves in clarifying the good or deducing what constitutes the conceptual basis of virtue. They have not usually been interested in vice, except as a conceptualistic medium to set virtue in clear relief. However, the ideological morality of Marxism-Leninism has had a much clearer plan for vice in its world-view (Ap. 65), based upon an empirical approach to *dynamic* involving a clear understanding of empirically dynamic forces like conscience. Once the vices of the enemies are empirically established, the revolutionary plan is to use them on two levels, (1) as they manifest themselves in the form of actual vices, and (2) as they manifest themselves in the form of incomplete virtues, which amount to the vices of omission.

In an instrumental morality where the only obligation is to preserve Marxist-Leninist ideology, the right must include the cultivation of any and all dynamic forces (even if they are vices) that could possibly help to gain the predetermined ends of Marxism (84:160, 161, 266). Furthermore, it is obligated to mobilize non-universal kinds of "good" that can be turned into vices through its more universal ideological tactics (84:95, 166, 171, 174, 177, 182, 202, 266) (Ap. 66).

The Empirical Approach to Dynamic.—In making a distinction between dynamic and static moral elements, Marxist-Leninists have been more empirical in their approach than Western thinkers. They have gone about first to separate the living from the dead, knowing that formalistic perfection alone does not witness to its own pragmatic effectiveness or its own need of empirical connections with the actual moral life of man. Since their interest is essentially in fact-creating, rather than merely in discursive, morality, ideologists in general have first distinguished the dynamic forces of history and then have channeled them by some form of a normative structure into "moral" patterns. They know that human forces, whether virtuous or vicious, are always creating something and that change is inevitable. Thus the first questions are, how to channel existing forces into moral patterns, and whether the theoretical framework will apply to existing forces that were moral issues before theory appeared on the scene.

To exemplify the empirical approach of an ideologist, we might use a dynamic (as well as stabilizing) empirical fact like conscience. From the fact of conscience, the ideologist would ideologically deduce dynamic factors (for example, the Christian ideologists like Paul deduced the decision always to serve the Creator rather than the creature [Romans 1:25]; the Marxist-Leninist ideologist would deduce the decision to give everything for the revolution). The ideological results would have to be logical (at least in some form sympathetic to his own world-view), but it is likely that the ideologist would refuse any sort of universality that was not empirically linked ideologically to actual dynamic forces of creativity (or even for the Marxist, destruction) (36:129). It is more relevant to human history, even if not to ethical formalism, to begin with a dynamic fact like love (or even for a Marxist, hate) and channel this into universal expression by moral pioneers (7:34; 32:272).

It is known among moral pioneers and professional moralists that there is higher pragmatic possibility of channeling a dynamic into something constructive, hate for instance, than there is of making certain well known ethical theories apply in the real world. Most theoretical systems have no adequate provision to deal with indifference (7:85, 87, 88, 96, 97), or temptations such as mediocrity and sloth. What could Kant do with those who have little or no "reverence" for the law? Or what could he do with those who have considerably dulled their own consciences?

An ideologist is first of all concerned with how much factual (i.e., empirical) *dynamic* can be deduced or created out of a basic dynamic moral factor (for example, love, hate). Then with his world-view he rejects all possible actions that are not maximum in the actual implementation of this world-view, even if they are logical. If from a dynamic factor such as conscience, he deduces an ideological obligation, then he must suspect or reject any deduction which lacks the *dynamic* of the first premise (conscience) even if it is (merely) logically consistent. The ideologists are not generally opposed to logical consistency (which is proved by the methodological acumen of Marxist-Leninists) but only to a consistency which is adverse or betraying to the dynamic factors which their basically dynamic empirical moral data implies; i.e., a basic *dynamic* like conscience ought to imply more than dead formality, even though it may imply a definite place for formal elements.

The whole question of ideological morality itself centers in corrigible history (as any relevant moral philosophy would) and man's part in it. What does not move social history is not a moral reality. Ideology works in a complementary but somewhat reverse

50

fashion from Aristotelian logic: the more universal a concept is, the more abstract and static; for ideology (as for Hegelian logic) the more comprehensive the universal, the greater its concreteness. In ideology, concentration is centered on the next step so that its world-view gives this particular step a concentrated *dynamic,* this *dynamic* being complementary to the moral universals to which the world-view may be attached. Ethical universals concerning the right in traditional philosophy are quasi-negatives and essentially tell us what not to do. And in this sense ideology needs them as a referee. But what checks the moral life or prevents it from deviating tangentially is not the same as that which gives it life, content, and ultimate direction.

By way of summary, the Marxist-Leninist revolutionary is a moral empiricist: he begins with an empirically dynamic element in human history and channels it suchwise that it becomes a contributing factor to a world-inclusive plan of history. He does this with the actual ideological virtues that have been mentioned in the second section of this chapter. This ideological ingenuity and inclusiveness are now shown by the revolutionary's ability to use the vices and even the partialistic virtues of his enemies. Let us consider the type of vices a Marxist-Leninist revolutionary can use to the advantage of his ideology (Ap. 67).

The Use of Vice.—The general characteristic of the type of vices that Marxist-Leninist revolutionaries have been able to channel into "virtues" sympathetic to their revolution are of two main types: (1) those that violate conscience, and (2) those that depend upon an incomplete conscience.

The vices that have violated the conscience involve dynamic fear of the light or the scrutiny of society. Examples of this type of vice include dishonesty, sexual impurity or perversion, or any activities that could contribute to scandal. The Marxist-Leninist revolutionary first finds out, with respect to the leadership of the enemy, their actual or potential moral failures of the light-resistant variety. If these vices are not sufficiently established, then the revolutionary helps his unwitting victim to cultivate them into conscience-crushing proportions (84:176, 177). This is done under the pretense of doing the victim a favor. Once this is established, then the process of blackmail begins to squeeze favors for the Marxist-

51

Leninist revolution from the victim. The victim is forced to co-operate or be exposed for his past, if simple favor trading will not work.

The second type of vice the Marxist-Leninist revolutionary uses successfully is the type that results from an incomplete conscience; that is, if one has a conscience that has resisted or neglected to deduce the implications of its moral axioms on an extensive or universal scale (a deduction that goes markedly beyond the point of self-interest), then his neglect can be used against him ideologically on both a tactical and strategic level.

Examples of this second type of vice (in religious language many of these would correspond to the sins of omission) would be the acts that would violate or fail to live up to a mature level of social sensitivity. A type in point is the situation in which an individual or social group has neglected to keep up with the times and its social needs. An example of this is isolationism, which was the American classical position stemming from Washington and Jefferson, and which is still held by a significant minority in this country. This may have been the most effective course for Washington and the early American nation; but in this era it is an unrealistic position, and in this sense a vice which the Marxist-Leninists are able to exploit. This is done through the tactic of causing internal dissention in order to weaken the solidarity of the free nations. This divisive tactic is insurance against the one thing which Marxist-Leninists hate to encounter, namely ideological solidarity among democratic peoples and nations. They cannot tolerate the coexistence of a better and rival ideology. Khrushchev said in 1958:

> In advocating peaceful coexistence, we, of course, have no intention of saying that there are no contradictions between socialism and capitalism, that complete "harmony" can be established between them, or that it is possible to reconcile the Communist and bourgeois ideologies. Such a viewpoint would be tantamount to retreating from Marxism-Leninism. The ideological differences are irreconcilable and will continue so. (9:125)

This implies that it is a "moral" necessity to agitate division among the enemy. Any trained Marxist-Leninist revolutionary is clever enough to accentuate the divisions that already exist through the blindness of an underdeveloped conscience or through the dynamic passion of personal hatreds (Ap. 68).

Although hatred can be subsumed among the former type of moral vice, it more often appears under the category of an incomplete or insensitive conscience. The revolutionary knows that among the most sophisticated type of democrats, hate is an unpleasant concept which is variously expressed through euphemisms, for example, "righteous indignation," or the suggestion "that one just doesn't neighbor very well." The revolutionary knows how to recognize and channel the *dynamic* of hate regardless of the names its possessors give it; he knows that these mild names do not do justice to the amount of passion in their possessors, but are likely to be euphemisms which indicate an insincere outgrowth of an incomplete or insensitive conscience which fails to see the implications of its own ideological blindness. When the consciences of democrats are less developed in their social implications than the Marxist-Leninist ideology is in revolutionaries, the door is open for the latter to channel these (morally unanalyzed) dynamic vices of their enemies into tendencies of social suicide. Indeed, according to Marxist-Leninist ethics, it is a moral ought for the revolutionary to do so.

Unless the conscience of democrats matches in self-consciousness and maturity the dynamic of Marxist-Leninist ideology, the adherents of democracy will have little capacity to resist the revolutionary drive to exploit social vices that exist in those who have an incomplete or insensitive conscience. Wherever liberal democrats neglect to make explicit and clear the theorems and corollaries of their own axioms of conscience, Marxist-Leninist revolutionaries will continue to create their own kind of ideological order. No matter what hate is called, it is still possible to channel it for insidious purposes, unless its possessors recognize that they are obligated to transform this *dynamic* into something morally coherent and constructive. The only alternative to having one's hate-dynamics exploited ideologically is first to decide to recognize them for what they are by their rightful names, since it is only on this basis that morally constructive decisions can follow to trans-

53

form them; only then can objectivity fulfill its obligation to reinforce, and be reinforced by, sincerity and sensitivity.

The Use of Incomplete Virtue.—One of the most effective moral tools of the Marxist-Leninist is the ideologically incomplete "virtues" of his enemy. These differ from vices of incomplete conscience (which are sometimes, although falsely, named and regarded as things that are morally neutral) by being considered as actual virtues by their possessors. Among such "virtues" are idealism, ambition, enlightened self-interest, friendship, nationalism, desire for adventure, and class consciousness, all of which have been used effectively and extensively by Marxist-Leninist revolutionaries (84: 168, 175). These virtues, it is true, have merit on their own level; but when they are not properly submissive to the more universal moral values and norms, they can be used destructively by revolutionaries with a more universally inclusive ideology.

Idealism is available for exploitation by revolutionaries when those who share it, never having faced the weaknesses and failures of their own human nature, exhibit a naive trust in those who speak their sympathetic and optimistic language, or rally uncritically to those who will aid their sectional cause (84:174, 175). The more sectional and fragmentary the idealism, the easier it is to subvert, particularly when this idealism is driven by a considerable amount of passion that is not channeled by an equal amount of personal ideological awareness.

When personal ambition, accepted in the capitalistic cultures as the mark of industry, becomes the driving force of a personality above the issue of what is right, then it becomes easy for revolutionaries to exploit it perversely in one way or another. Ravines fed the ambition of a few as the wedge to split the radicals in Chile. It is generally the case that any "virtue" which consistently allows its possessors to use other men as a means condemns itself to ideological usury. Mores that result from sectionalism or class consciousness are no match for a more universal ideology.

The Human Goals of Marxist-Leninist Morality

A major point of distinction in Marxist-Leninist morality is the central position of its very definite human goals; and on this basis it might be classified scientifically as a process theory of ethics (T. E. Hill), and treated as a goal-directed system. Although the communist system regards itself as "scientific," such a treatment of it would be irrelevant, because it is an ideology. If it proclaims the "inevitability of history," it nonetheless embodies volitional principles that in ordinary language are spoken of as a hope, a faith, or an ideological goal (Ap. 48). This goal has human implications found in few of the synoptic Western philosophical ethical systems, and scarcely at all in the more analytic approaches, except in a vague non-empirical, not readily applicable form. This creative communist principle is the new type of man, which, as eschatological in nature, is alien to a merely scientific approach or discursive treatment.

The New Type of Man.—Contrary to Kantian humanism, whose ideal man was transcendent, and whose perfection was to be achieved solely by himself, Marxist-Leninist humanism is identified totally with this world and mankind is to be perfected by collective action. Where Kant appealed to moral reason in the individual, Marx and Lenin believed that the new man of the coming classless society, who would possess freedom and dignity in his own dialectical (i.e. peculiar) way, could only be fashioned by force into a completely social man who would no longer need (at some unexplainable point of the dialectic of history) the use of force. This re-creating of man was to be done within the framework of the factories, i.e. within the right mode of production (5:102, 127).

The 1960 *History of the C.P.S.U.*, however, speaks of the creation of the new man in somewhat broader terms:

> The Congress pointed out that it was of exceptional importance for the building of Communism to raise the political consciousness and activity of the masses, to educate the working people in a Communist spirit. At the present stage emphasis in Communist education was laid on the moulding of the new man, on the education of politically conscious workers of Communist society. The task of the Party and the State in the ideological field was to develop new qualities in Soviet people, to educate them in the spirit of collectivism and industriousness, Socialist internationalism and patriotism, and in steadfast observance of the lofty principles of Communist morality. (86:726)

This more recent approach to the new man is more explicitly ideological than the earlier, because it appeals to outspoken idealism in terms of "lofty principles." This idealism, however, is not philosophical (i.e. metaphysical or ontological) ; it is an ideological idealism which is a natural outgrowth of the increasing totalism of scope in Russian ideological methodology. Marx's ideology was still in the pre-natal stage, and therefore he was not empirically aware of the necessary breadth of an activistic philosophy (i.e. an ideology) which possesses adequate human *dynamic*. Here Lenin was more profound, being far more pragmatic about the necessary ideological means even though he retained Marx's goals. Stalin, Khrushchev, and the present regime, as late party literature has exhibited, have advanced this ideological idealism even further.

The goal of Marxist-Leninist morality, a communist society which is officially identified with the formula of "From each according to his ability, to each according to his needs" (86:726) , is really a society to be composed of the new type of man. The Marxist, of course, did not create this model of humanity, but they are accepting it more seriously than are most of their philosophical rivals.

Without the hope of the new man, Marxism-Leninism would lose much of its moral force. Power in this system is generated primarily by the extensiveness of its ideology and its superior ability to harness and utilize a wide variety of human dynamic forces. Its ideology, masked as an embodiment of dialectical logic, allows its revolutionaries to exploit evil as well as good will in the pursuit of their scheme to create the new man (5:183) . The effectiveness of this ethos is indicated by the Marxist-Leninist revolutionaries themselves, who are a quasi-new type of man for whom ordinary notions of morality are alien; they are dynamic men who contrast remarkably to the average Western hedonist or religionist. Nonetheless the "new man" is not emerging in Russia as rapidly as was expected, and its leadership has acknowledged this fact. At a late Party Congress the question was raised as to why the new man was so tardy in appearing (14:8) .

Even though the new man is late in appearing, the Marxist-Leninists are still persistent in creating the conditions necessary for his arrival, of which one basic condition is putting first things first. The new man is a social, not an individualistic man; "public interests come before all others" (86:628). Individual men are a means to attaining the new level of social mankind. In that Marxist-Leninist morality is instrumental itself, its consistency does not lie in a moral consistency, like Kant's, in treating individuals wholly as ends. Moreover it is an inverted ideological consistency of always considering the individual as a means. Every human *dynamic* or social force is to be channeled in this fashion. Consequently, putting first things first is to use particular men to produce the "men of the future" (84:179). Each man must learn, through a "world outlook," "to use all the media of ideological work" (86: 742).

In the choice of these media is revealed the real outworking of Marxist-Leninist moral theory in the actual world. The most unique aspect of this morality is the idea that the pathway to good is not only through other instrumental goods, but also through evil. This is justified by the greatest of all Marxist-Leninist metaphysical leaps, that evil will pass into good if it serves the revolution. Because the new man is a social generality, no individual moral conscience is allowed to challenge extensively the dialectical use of evil (5:183). This is illustrated by Mao Tse-tung's description of the *Yenan Way;* when Ravines raised the question about the morality ("faulty") of certain means, the former replied,

> Oh comrade! You are going back to the cave from which I've tried to draw you! Most faulty? Least faulty? Free from defects? No, that is not the most essential thing. You must judge coldly who serves the party and who fails to serve it. This must be your only criterion. Remember that all our concessions are only temporary. Don't forget that we communists are fighting for the world revolution. When it triumphs the steel columns of communism will march over the bodies of those same people who now hasten to offer us their protection. It can not be helped. It is an inescapable consequence! . . .
> Our goal is to make ourselves strong, to acquire skill in mass action, to win positions and become capable later of striking blows. (84.161)

What allows Marxist-Leninists to parade such goal-directed ideology, masqueraded as a form of logic, is the dialectical concept of "consistency." If such "consistency" is alien to the traditional scientific concepts of non-contradiction, it is nonetheless an operative fact which moral philosophy must take into account. This new volitional consistency is a refusal to compromise on the final goal.

The basic moral difference between Marxist-Leninist socialism and the other varieties of socialism is its refusal to compromise about its strategy. The 1960 official *History of the C.P.S.U.* expresses this point:

> The C.P.S.U., which was founded by the great Lenin, is a party of a new type. Unlike the reformist and Social Democratic parties, parties of the old type that follow a policy of compromise and reconciliation of the proletariat with the bourgeoisie, the Communist Party expresses the fundamental interests of the proletariat as a class fighting for the triumph of Socialist revolution, for the abolition of the exploiting system, for the creation of a Socialist and a Communist society. (86:745)

The basic foundation for this no-compromise policy is that Marxism-Leninism is a world outlook with a definite plan for every phase and part of it, expressed in the proposition that there is a "right orientation in any situation" (Ap. 69).

The New World.—The Marxist-Leninist "world outlook" has a moral extensiveness and breadth of application that makes many of the traditional world-views look fragmentary by comparison. This is why Marxist-Leninist morality has such strong sanctions or dynamic force, in spite of its unconvincing "logic." This ideological morality, to date, has avoided much of the petrification of Western moralities because it has not allowed ethics to become a private affair. In this respect it serves to stress the fact that no socially consistent world-outlook is compatible with the claim that morality is a private affair; extreme individualism, by its very nature, cannot be a truly coherent world-outlook.

Nevertheless, the idea "that morality is a private affair" is one of the chief ideological tools used by Marxist-Leninist revolutionaries to divide the moral and ideological solidarity of its enemies; for example, an effective tactic is to foster the idea that religion and morality have no necessary relationship. As an ideological tool, this divorce of religion and morality allows the victim to substitute what he wants, in a religious garb, for what is right, in the form of the false equation, "What I want (if consistent to my own religious creed) equals what is right." In this ideologically clever way Marxist-Leninist revolutionaries help and abet religion to become "the opiate of the people" among their enemies; for it is the case, ideologically speaking, that religion which falls short of ideological completeness in its account of man or the world is an opiate at least by way of default.

A religion without absolute moral standards (24:186) may similarly become an opiate; for, in the words of H. J. Paton, "No man is religious unless he is seeking the good life" (79:63). This ideological concept of absolute standards is not an abstract absolute; it is a practical one. As B. Lund Yates aptly puts it,

> . . . the first step to faith is the restoration of absolute moral standards. This is not a theoretical question of the possibility of an absolute in morals, or even in the first instance the proposal that a man should adopt moral standards to which he has not previously subscribed; it is primarily a practical question. It is a question of applying to himself uncompromisingly and absolutely the moral standards which a man already recognizes with the roots of his being. And this is a question of willingness. (98:3)

One who lets his moral standards move with convenience may possess a theory, but he has no standard. A standard must stand, and in this sense it holds absolutely, without exceptions of convenience. Moral absolutes are not a question of metaphysical ultimates since man cannot be held morally responsible for what is merely speculative, nor are they a question of a fixed and absolute mental conception which allows no advance in the realm of moral cognition. These "absolutes" are moreover the consistent refusal to give one's self the luxury to compromise with the full scope of one's own present moral world-view; they are the refusal to indulge in the basic insincerity of not compelling one's self without exception to live the life of what C. I. Lewis calls "reasonableness" (54:87).

Marxist-Leninist revolutionaries know that a world-view without any absolute moral standards, which in Kantian terminology is limited to hypothetical rather than categorical imperatives, is no match ideologically for a world-view that does have them and consequently can make moral demands on the public. Even an ideology which claims that social progress is under way cannot provide for genuine and sustained moral response unless it provides for an imperative principle absolutely binding on the individual, whether this be dialectical necessity, . . . or God's will. These revolutionaries have capitalized on the lack of clarity on this point among all of their enemies, whose lack of a genuine and morally binding world outlook has contributed considerably to present communistic success.

The Marxist-Leninist drive to re-make the world includes stress on, and exploitation of, the revolutionary will (5:150), the demands upon which comprise much of what is called scientific inevitability (9:86). The success of this drive, up to the present, exhibits the extraordinary power possessed by ideological volition, and, at the same time, the profound danger such a principle can be to free inquiry and the right of philosophical criticism. What gives it power here is its systematization in a manner to make it available in all areas of action. This technology of will is not based on the descriptive approach of much Western psychology; it is identified, rather, with the ability of the revolutionaries to channel it effectively, once *dynamic* has been generated ideologically by a clear goal and a totalistic world-view. In this achievement lies the secret of ideological genius.

The danger of this Marxist-Leninist exaltation of will lies in the fact that no moral norms are provided by means of which it can be independently judged. Morality in this system is demonic; it is exclusively instrumental, and is appraised exclusively in terms of effective or ineffective service to the ideological goal which is held to be an implicit fact of history. Marxist-Leninists, however, have failed to learn from history the consequences of their position, namely, that once a belief is paraded as fact, the door is opened wide to injustice of the most grotesque and excessive kinds; of which two examples, among an innumerable class of historical facts, are the Renaissance Inquisition and recent Nazism. It is, of course, true that the application of this vicious confusion between certified truth and belief in the revolution is the source of its success; but this success has been purchased at the price of dialectical contradiction which will always threaten the moral fibre of communist cultures. Meanwhile the only effective deterrent against this wilful perversion, i.e., the identification of belief and fact, and the forcing of belief upon others as truth (for example, the belief that evil will become good), is to counter it with a better world-view or ideology. This superior ideology must be a moral one, and it must work in harmony with the best in science; it can then generate force of will and effectively direct it, without dishonor to human dignity and the value of free choice. Such an ideology would never parade belief or faith as "fact," nor would it seek to justify the use of persons as mere means. Its *dynamic* would result from a proper co-relation of belief and fact, of will and intellect, not their identification.

Western thinkers have not commonly adopted the view, whether in public or private morality, that the will as such is above the intellect; but they have in general failed to consider seriously the nature of will in its ideological expressions and the effective means to control it. Prior to the present century religion has been more successful than technical philosophy has been in re-channeling individual wills; and on the social level it may well be that it alone can be expected to do so. But in the present atomic age, in which Western liberal culture is challenged by alien and illiberal systems that embody vicious elements, only religion that possesses an adequate ideology can be adequate to the responsibilities now imposed upon it. Such an effective religion (and I have Christianity specifically in mind) involves two characteristics essential in this connection. On the one hand, facing an alien colossus of Marxist-Leninist ideology which makes morality a subordinate means, not an autonomous principle with its own criteria of judgment, it must accept absolute morality of independent principles. On the other hand, as religion it must abandon most of its excess baggage of theological dogma of the Greek intellectualistic tradition which has little or no direct purpose in re-making men in the apostolic sense.

Scientific psychology is likewise not adequately equipped to do this; it does not comprehend the field of normative values, hence, final goals, nor can it provide the *dynamic* that sustains the will effectively enough to attain these goals. A sustained drive toward a morally adequate future will require the free world to meet the threat of alien ideological moralities with a morally superior ideology; this is essentially a relational approach involving a dynamic co-operation of the highest forms of knowledge and belief (including values), belief and action, action (will) and knowledge (intellect), the descriptive and normative on a universal scale. This is the unique service of a moral philosophy which is comprehensive enough to include a vital relationship to a moral ideology.

CHAPTER 4

THE NATURE OF A MORAL IDEOLOGY

Since 'ideology,' like 'philosophy,' is a word with considerable fluidity and lack of standard meaning, I propose to define a moral ideology as: a dynamic, methodological approach to mobilizing will on both a particular and a universal scale in order to change history on the basis of a world-view subjected to universal moral norms. In analytic terms, the absolutely essential elements are (1) a *dynamic*, (2) a world-view, which includes a view of the nature of man, and (3) a methodology capable of attaining its philosophical ends (Ap. 70, 71). These elements are the relational links between knowledge, justified belief, and action (Ap. 1), forming them into a cognitively balanced whole capable of sustaining dynamic morality on a scale commensurate with the universality of the highest norms.

The world-view is a synthesis of knowing and believing, the *dynamic* is a synthesis of believing and doing, and the methodology is a synthesis of doing and knowing. Just as an epistemological approach to moral cognition requires a methodological separating of knowing, believing, and doing, a moral ideology requires a synthetic combining of these elements to form its world-view, *dynamic,* and methodology. Similarly, it requires the proper synoptic interaction of these latter factors to constitute its pragmatic effectiveness and moral integrity.

The Element of a Dynamic

Dynamic in Critical Thinking.—The dynamic element, or passion, of an ideology is positive in regard to its scientific respectability (Ap. 72) even though there has been an abundance of scientifically unrespectable and dangerously subjective ideologies. Where ideological *dynamic* is necessary at all, it is even more essential to the critical thinker than it is to the naive realist who gullibly embraces the panaceas of sub-moral ideologies; the critical thinker must often brave the currents and winds of prejudice whereas the naive realist needs only to allow himself to be swept along by the currents of unquestioned custom or mass psychology. In fact, scientific discovery itself has flowered upon what Hocking describes as the effort of scientists "to achieve a passionate respect for dispassionate fact" (31:462). Polanyi goes even further in stating the dynamic role of intellectual passions:

> Intellectual passions do not merely affirm the existence of harmonies which foreshadow an indeterminate range of future discoveries, but can also evoke intimations of specific discoveries and sustain their persistent pursuit through years of labour. The appreciation of scientific value merges here into the capacity for discovering it; even as the artist's sensibility merges into his creative powers. Such is the heuristic function of scientific passion. (80:143)

If science is both justified and also obligated at times to include a dynamic element (for example, a passion toward objectivity or discovery), then it should be self-evident that something as will-centered as a moral ideology would be totally ineffective without it.

Parallel to Charles Gillispie's statement that "things in motion . . . are what science studies" (25:44), I maintain that united wills in motion are what ideology studies. By definition it is the dynamic element which is synonymous with either the setting of the will into motion or, at least, the removing of obstacles to a will that would otherwise be in motion. Therefore, since a moral ideology is a methodological approach, the use of *dynamic* indicates the actual systematic and organized uniting of wills on the basis of moral principles.

Dynamic in Ancient Philosophy.—In Western civilization these dynamic elements which set wills into motion have been present for many centuries. Socrates was one of the first to give *dynamic* an academic status by pointing out that much of the strivings (i.e. wills in motion) of men were after the wrong things. He admonished men to strive after the Good, leading the way himself by means of the dynamic direction of his "daemon" who taught him his mission in the world. In the *Apology*, he reveals his dynamic attitude:

> —if this was the condition on which you let me go, I should reply: Men of Athens, I honour and love you; but I shall obey God rather than you, and while I have life and strength I shall never cease from the practice and teaching of philosophy, exhorting any one whom I meet . . . (*Apol.* 29)

This dynamic element was not recaptured in Western thinking until the Christians expounded the concept of the Holy Spirit.

With Plato, *dynamic* became academic and transcendent. With Aristotle, it became totally overshadowed by his respect for the "unmoved"; nevertheless it regained a certain philosophical status through his pupil Alexander the Great. R. C. Mowat gives an excelent analysis of the role ideological *dynamic* played during this time of conquest:

> Alexander's world was a world of ideological conflict. The conflicts of ideas which raged among the Greeks were complicated by the clash between Greek ideas and those coming from Persia, Egypt, and other civilizations. The old faith of the Greeks gave way to mystical or atheistic philosophies, and to adaptations of oriental religions.
>
> Each Greek state, too, developed its own particular patriotic faith, while Greeks in their relations with non-Greeks were animated by strong feelings of racial and cultural superiority. Such feelings could issue in what we might term an ideology, in the sense of a faith which sets into motion not merely individuals but entire peoples. Such elements are to be found in the faith of Alexander, who believed he had a divine vocation to spread his orientalised version of the Greek way of life throughout the world. (70:124, 125)

With or without philosophical justification, Alexander possessed the *dynamic* to mobilize will on a scale unequaled before his time; his use of ideological force was more *dynamic* than moral, yet his diffusion of Greek culture has not been without its lasting benefits.

The Christian Source of Dynamic Morality.—Christianity has been the fountain-head of the concept of 'the need of moral *dy-*

namic in human history'; this is exemplified in its unparalleled centralizing of *'agape'* and 'grace.' Bergson has given considerable insight concerning the uniqueness of this dynamic ("open") element in human conduct and its relation to Christianity:

> There seems to be no doubt that this second advance, the passage from the closed to the open, is due to Christianity, as the first was due to the Prophets of Judaism. Could it have been brought about by mere philosophy? There is nothing more instructive than to see how the philosophers have skirted round it, touched it, and yet missed it. (7:77)

This dynamic moral force, according to Bergson, is "an impetus in the realm of the will" (7:48) ; it appears in the form of elements, like Christian *agape,* which are capable of bridging the wide gap between intellectual assent and the transformation of the will. *Dynamic* with the power to transform the will is not anti-intellectual, but it does possess a supra-rational consistency of its own (foreign to intellectualism) which becomes rational in historical retrospect; many of the Biblical writings are the crystallizations of these dynamic forces (Ap. 73) . It was not long, however, until Biblical dynamism was overshadowed by Greek intellectualism; Scholasticism was the result.

Modern Intellectualism and Dynamic Morality.—If anything seemingly was to render moral *dynamic* irrelevant to philosophy, it was Newtonian physics; even though physics dealt with power and motion, its determinism necessarily excluded the human will. The successes of physics have lured philosophy into emulating its dispassionate exactness even in subjects like ethics, for example where men like Spinoza excluded all passion through his geometrical approach. Much of this scientistic emulation was based upon the mistake of confusing all human dynamic elements with mere emotion or irrationality. Though it is true that moral *dynamic* is more difficult to systematize or rationalize, it is a scientistic mistake to assume that all dynamic elements in philosophy or ideology are mere emotion or that they have a necessary connection with irrationality.

Dynamic Gains New Philosophical Status.—Hume sought to counter this rationalistic extreme by his claim that common to all mankind are the "generous sentiments" which have even the power to overcome self-love, thus giving human *dynamics* a definite role in moral philosophy. Kant went even further in giving a dynamic element like obligation a philosophical status by calling it "the sole fact of pure reason," even though he never clarified the sense in which it is a fact. Here Kant unadmittedly stands on ideology and philosophizes therefrom. In spite of his neglect of the importance of many value commitments (94:357, 360), he did show in his emphasis on "making room for faith" that there are certain dynamic elements in ethics that scientific understanding does not encompass. The dynamic elements which Kant preserved for philosophy were given a fully ideological status in the absolute idealism of Fichte and Hegel, which centered in the spiritual development of the person rather than in the knowledge of being. Here they went beyond Kant's position, that the "idea of duty" out of "respect" (94:354) was the only adequate moral motivation, into a host of dynamic categories virtually unknown in previous academic philosophy.

The French Revolutionary Thinkers Use Ideology as a Dynamic Weapon.—It was the French revolutionary thinkers who began to give the dynamic elements in ideology significant attention in their practical implications, but their failure was in the realm of philosophy in the form of a perverting reductionism. Nevertheless, a man like Diderot showed his ideological ability in the realm of methodology and *dynamic* by devising a means to use the dynamic force of men's interest and respect for technology to propel his ideology (25:174). His aim was to change the general way of thinking with his *Encyclopedia* by making much ideology appear like science, and thus capitalize upon the gullibility of men who believed his ideas and were thereby under the dynamic expectation that this ideological revolution would bring tangible results like those the new science had brought. It was here that ideology had taken an immoral turn in parading belief as fact.

Dynamic Elements in the Modern World.—Since Hegel and the French ideologues, the ideological forces have found a considerable part of their *dynamic* in the form of reaction against some real or alleged fact or condition. With the Nazis, it was a reaction against Jews and other "inferior" peoples; with Marxist-Leninists, it is presently a *dynamic* fanned by the hate against the "evils" that property and theism create. The amazing thing about all of this is that these irrational *dynamics* have captivated the minds of great multitudes, inspiring a sense of duty that exceeds the effects of some of the best academic, philosophical moralities. (For a detailed analysis of Marxist-Leninist use of *dynamic,* see "The Empirical Approach to *Dynamic"* in chapter 3.)

Bergson's Distinction between Impulsion and Attraction.— Bergson shows a penetrating insight into this seemingly unjustified failure of current moral philosophies:

> In order to define the very essence of duty, we have in fact distinguished the two forces that act upon us, impulsion on the one hand, and attraction on the other. This had to be done, and it is because philosophy had left it undone, confining itself to the intellectuality which to-day covers both, that it has scarcely succeeded, so it would seem in explaining how a moral motive can have a hold upon the souls of men. (7:65)

What Bergson is saying is that impulsion is a form of "pressure"; attraction, the other side of the coin, is a form of "aspiration." Philosophical conceptualization has compounded these two factors into a blend, without realizing the essential differences. The majority of philosophical theories of duty have lacked proper *dynamic* because of their inability to see the distinction between pressure and aspiration, impulsion and attraction, the social and the supersocial (7:65, 66). In the ordinary moral situations one does not split himself into two selves, but his realization that both of these factors exist in him, and the ability to distinguish them, creates a much better key to moral effectiveness; the effectiveness is the result of a proper balance of the factors of pressure and aspiration in light of the particular issues confronting him. The attainment of this proper balance of the static with the dynamic elements is not a matter of set proportion but a matter of wisdom and moral artistry, which only comes through the realization of the importance of both factors in the moral life. This is at the heart of an effective moral ideology. In the last 150 years, there have been an abundance of moral philosophies that were highly intellectual but ineffective;

worse yet, men have experienced great ideological forces that have been *dynamic* but immoral. Moral philosophy will be no more unscientific if it begins to recognize its relationship to the dynamic forces of 'wills in motion' (ideology) than physics is by studying the means to harness atomic energy. Human survival may well depend upon a proper sense of relation between these three factors: ideological *dynamic,* moral principles, and atomic energy. It will take ideological *dynamic* (or something at least equivalent) to apply moral principles strongly enough to inspire responsible use of atomic energy.

The Proper Relation between Fixed and Changing Elements.— The basic implication of the position that morality has a dynamic side is that change is an essential moral category. Principles are fixed, things change. Man is in the middle and he is responsible to himself and to the world in recognizing that change will come; it is only a matter of choosing the best kinds of change that will not violate his highest principle. He must see that it is not a question of whether he changes, but *how* he changes, that is, how he responds to new circumstances. His new responses to new circumstances are new factors in his character, and the presence of these in themselves implies the continual occurrence of change. Even wilful indifference to moral factors implies change in the way of added impetus to moral insensitivity. The moral agent cannot escape making a decision; and as C. I. Lewis says, "failure of decision is itself a manner of deciding" (52:5, 6) .

The Basic Issue Is How the Dynamic Forces Are Guided.— In some way all men are being swept along by the great river of transition, and where possible, they must guide the transition or be at the mercy of circumstance. The meaning of the concept 'changed man' essentially consists in the way the man in question responds to moral circumstances; circumstances change, and the morally transformed man should be capable of directing these dynamic forces into morally acceptable channels through his realization of the proper relation of knowledge (the stabilizing element) and faith (the dynamic element) . To gain such a relational balance he must reject opportunistic motives of success which cause him to parade faith as knowledge, and also any desires for security which cause him to neglect the explicit role of belief or faith ("Any knowing must include belief in something not sense-given but credited as authentic" [52:26]). All ideologies use belief or faith as their basic dynamic force, including Russian Marxism. Mowat says,

> Marxism in Russia has fused with this particular national, or rather supranational ideology, which is her secularized inheritance from her Christian past. It is this which makes Russian communism such a dynamic—and demonic—force in the modern world. (70:143)

The immoral ideologies parade belief as knowledge and then use the "compulsion" of physical force; on the contrary, a moral ideology finds even more dynamic force by admitting belief openly and mobilizing human will by "attraction."

The way "dynamic by attraction" works will be treated in chapter 6.

The Element of a World-View

With social unity as a necessary goal, the world-view of a moral ideology (a synthesis of knowing and value-beliefs) extends only into the realm of where men must make decisions; hence a moral ideology necessarily presupposes an understanding of the reciprocal relationship between ideological objectivity and decision, which, in turn, begets a balanced relation of essentials.

The Goal of Unity.—In order to be both ideologically adequate and morally competent, the world-view of a moral ideology must have a clear and singleminded goal which leads toward a noble kind of social unity. It is a unity of spirit which comes not merely from the lack of something on which to disagree, but upon the volitional agreement that men should act as if they need the help of other minds. C. I. Lewis reinforces this conviction philosophically by saying,

> Two heads are better than one—and this not merely because two heads may contain more information. Beyond that, it reflects the obverse of a fact already noted: unanimity is a fair index of correctness, since errors are likely to be various.

> There is the same need to submit moral findings of the individual to the social consensus that there is to check our logical conclusions and our mathematical demonstrations, whose correctness likewise is a matter which does not turn upon empirical information. (54:95, 96)

Even though there must be the relation of conceptual unity between the individuals possessing a common world-view, there also must be the relation to actual unity through right action;

> a way of acting, to be right in a given case, must be one which would, in the same premises of action, be right in every instance and right for anybody. (54:93)

The world-view of a moral ideology, after establishing conceptual unanimity about the content of basic human decision, must proceed to its volitional implication through systematic action.

The world-view of a moral ideology is prescriptive as well as descriptive; consequently it must imply a coherent process from what *is* to what *ought* to be. In philosophical world-views the process toward their goals, i.e., the means of gaining their ends, is often the morally weak element even though the goals in themselves may be morally acceptable. Since the attainment of the ultimate goals of a moral ideology is usually considerably remote, it is the process or means of advancement that may cause most of the moral friction; therefore a moral ideology must develop its world-view in such a way that its methodological process is not only theoretically consistent but also volitionally consistent with the moral principles and attitudes that all men of good will would hold. In other words, a process toward an ideological goal must involve a moral consistency in its norms of pragmatic instrumentalism, as well as theoretical consistency in the norms of its final goals; but in philosophical ethics the theoretical too often considerably outbalances the pragmatic. Examples of norms that approach a better philosophical balance are, 'always maximize value,' or 'always be reasonable (i.e., always *do* what is known to be right).' These norms rightly imply that there is a pragmatic as well as a theoretical gap between what does exist in the social area and what ought to exist; the 'ought' includes the pragmatic implication that action is neces-

71

sary on some level, even if it is the wilful activity of patient waiting. The world-view of a moral ideology must include the pragmatic, i.e. a philosophical recognition of action, since it is neither more nor less than a philosophy of unity which must be created by decision.

The Nature of Ideological Decision.—Without concerted decision, a moral ideology would amount to a mere conceptualization about action. To a real ideologist, a decision about the normative goals of a moral world-view is markedly different from an axiological or a conceptualistic desire; decision is usually founded upon the desire of a felt-value, but desire alone is not a decision (for details see chapter 6) .

In addition to possessing its own unique characteristics, decision is inescapable. Even though most of man's crucial decisions are limited to the foundation of well-reasoned *belief,* decision itself must remain central in a moral ideology, otherwise the fact of decision on crucial issues will go by default into the hands of irrational ideologies. A moral ideology must know the relationship of decision to its body of knowledge, value norms, and beliefs. Especially it must know the rank of order in which decisions are to be made, since the order of decision in a particular ideology gives considerable insight into its morality. It is the centralizing of decision that makes the world-view of a moral ideology different from most other philosophical world-views.

A moral ideology is a philosophy of united decision and thereby the persuading of men to make decisions upon well-reasoned belief and knowledge, rather than upon something less. After all, philosophical proof itself cannot escape the use of persuasion. C. I. Lewis says,

> It is of the essence of the dialectical or reflective method that we should recognize that proof, in philosophy, can be nothing more at bottom than persuasion. It makes no difference what the manner of presentation should be, whether deductive from initial assumptions, or inductive from example, or merely following the order dictated by clarity of exposition . . .
>
> There can be no Archimedean point for the philosopher. Proof, he can offer only in the sense of so connecting his theses as to exhibit their mutual support, and only through

appeal to other minds to reflect upon their experience and
their own attitudes and perceive that he correctly portrays
them. (53:23)

The persuasion of a moral ideology concerns the issues that are
matters of reasonableness, responsibility, and the challenge to men
to honor the highest values in all their choices. (It is the area of
common inclusion of the spheres of knowing, valuing, and doing
in Appendix 1.)

Since its world-view is one of united decision toward unity, a
moral ideology will have benefited the world if it is able to persuade
mankind to make the decision to seek an international morality.
Radoslav Tsanoff says, "the attainment of an international morality
is the greatest need of our time" (92:14). I believe that only the
world-view of a moral ideology is capable of the necessary balance
of the conceptual and the decisional needed to effect such a persuasion. It is unfortunate that contemporary ethical philosophers
have tended to leave the business of persuasion to "professional
moralists" without having any clear concept of whether the so-
called "professionals" are able to do the job that has been thrown
to them like "scraps from the master's table." It is not very reasonable to leave such an important task as international morality to
professional moralists unless they have the tools to succeed. If they
work in an ideological age like this one, the professional moralists
cannot succeed in their role of persuasion and training unless they
have an ideological world-view that is more comprehensive and
effective than the immoral ideologies that they must encounter. To
date, a great many of the professional moralists have been opportunistic individualists, and, as such, have had little effect in curing
human selfishness. Hence non-dictatorial persuasion on an international level is the business of a moral ideology.

The objective of ideological decision in its persuasive role is
'that which is beyond point of view,' i.e. on 'what is right'; unless
the right is the central objective of an ideology, it has no alternative
but to be a program of using its own point-of-view to exclude other
points-of-view. On any lesser basis than right-centered objectivity,
it will amount only to a process of rearranging the prejudices of
others in the same sense that scientism and much creed-centered religion operate. The world-view of a moral ideology must seek that

which is beyond point-of-view as the counterpart to the strivings for objectivity in science; as a philosophy of decision it must be open-ended, i.e. its commitment toward truth must supersede any opinion it may include. It must be open to the idea that new data in the moral realm may appear, obligating a complete reappraisal of any and all its own ends and methods. In fact, the world-view of a moral ideology is more correctly a world attitude that cannot tolerate even a sentimental tenacity to its own conceptual world-view, being necessarily able to discard parts of its own intellectual framework in order to inspire others not to be bound as victims of their own point-of-view. It is a decisional world-view which must continually decide to accept and embrace what is right on the basis of the "value commitments of a civilized humanity" (94:5) regardless of the change it requires. It must be a clear analysis of the general status of human need based on the best available facts and inspired by the most noble forms of justified belief; and, above all, it must avoid becoming too speculative since this would render it immoral as a philosophy of action, because human lives should not be used as a means of speculative experimentation.

The Nature of Ideological Objectivity.—There is just one predetermined goal of a moral ideology, and that is morality. The only alternative for an ideological world-view to distinctions made on the basis of color, class, race, etc., is that ideology must be finally responsible to moral norms; consequently, it must take a provisional attiude toward all points-of-view. As a philosophy of action, it must hold to the principle that its business is to change men and society, but as a moral world-view, it must allow ethics to provide unmovable standards that will not sway with human whims and motives. This is a question of 'what is right' in any given issue rather than the relativism of 'who is right' based on point-of-view. Being a philosophy of both particular and universal action, the world-view of a moral ideology must be clear on how to begin by applying particular moral remedies to particular social situations on the basis of acceptable moral standards.

Since it is often the case that the moral battle-lines in society are already formed by the morally incompetent ideologies, a basic objective of a moral ideology must be to draw the battle-line in the right place according to the universally valid moral norms, rather than upon point-of-view as the Marxists and Nazis have done. 'Universally valid' does not imply some abstract, immovable, metaphysical absolute; it simply means the best that men know to date. In order to remain an ideology as well as a moral world-view, however, a moral ideology must be willing to strive for the objectivity of what is right, and in order to remain moral it must draw the battle-line somewhere; the question is *where*. Immoral ideologies draw theirs on the basis of something less than character: the Nazis based their ideology on division of race, using race consciousness to justify their acts of aggression; the Marxists have been considerably more inclusive in basing their division of humanity along class lines, giving them the advantage over Nazism through their appeal to the workers, the majority of humanity, whom they call upon to unite. But on the other hand, a moral ideology must recognize the dignity of all men beyond the divisions of race, class, color, or creed. Then the question may be asked as to what valid distinction is there left for man to decide about, and for ideology to persuade? The answer is shockingly simple, but not a triviality; it is the distinction between good will and evil will; it is a question of character, and not race or class. An ideology based on anything less is immoral.

There is at least one point where the world-view of a moral ideology must be dogmatic: if, as ideologists, men want change of character to come in others, they must have the objectivity of character to begin with themselves. This is an inverted type of dogmatism from that of authoritarianism, since it is not so much a dogma about alleged facts as it is about a normative attitude. It is the attitude that the moral battle-line in the world is not essentially about our factual opinions (since our "facts" and theories may so easily be wrong or superseded) but about one's ideological perspective of where to begin, as the proper foundation of the goal of our moral encounter. Only as the adherents of an ideological world-view begin with themselves do they manifest the moral realization that the moral battle-line must (unless they have attained perfection) cut right through every particular individual or group; any moral norm that does not first reveal "where I or my group must change" is inadequate to guide a moral ideology in its business of taking others as directly as possible toward 'what' is right.

Humanity is overflowing with the subconscious illusion that "things would be in very good order if all men were like us," which necessarily implies that to do what is right in some way would involve a necessary move toward "our point-of-view." Even if it were the case that to do right would involve moving toward "our point-of-view," such would be coincidental to the fact "our point-of-view" was moving toward, or was reasonably near, some objective moral standard; but this would likely reveal the weakness of the standard rather than "our" perfection. On the other hand the endeavor toward what is right (i.e. ideological objectivity) would be, by its very nature, to point others beyond "what we have attained," and it would be with the realization that to take others toward what is right will necessarily not be straight toward "our point-of-view."

The need of ideological objectivity is more easily described by an illustration in the field of religion; for example, if a man is a conservative in his theological outlook, he may be strongly inclined to believe that, if a liberal is to move toward God in his religious experience, then the liberal must come to God by way of becoming a conservative. He does this because he has wrongly put the question of point-of-view above 'what is right.' The religious man who lives by 'what is right' allows those of a different point-of-view to approach God in the most direct way possible from where the other man is, and not via the former's point-of-view. A sincere theist realizes that God is the Truth, and Truth can never be limited to his point-of-view, even though he may participate in the Truth.

In summary, the basis of objectivity necessary to the world-view of a moral ideology is that those who adhere to such an ideology are responsible to begin this advance toward universal norms by changing themselves first. Ideology based upon anything less is both dangerous and insincere.

A Balanced Relation of Essentials.—Cognitively speaking, the essentials of the world-view (i.e. the cognitive scheme) of a moral ideology are knowledge, justified belief (including a scale of values), and action (i.e. decision or intention).

Knowledge, if it is to play its proper role in an ideological world-view, must be non-speculative and essentially modest in its cognitive claims. When the ideologist indulges in speculative luxuries under the name of knowledge, he is well on the way to

76

using ideology as an immoral weapon of coercion. It is possible to avoid speculation by staying within a proper sense of ideological order and priority; for example, ideological knowledge, as it includes the best of scientific knowledge, must also relate in a definite way to the decisional concept of remaking men and nations through knowing the very next moral phase of advancement for a particular man or nation. It must be anti-speculative in the sense that any step but the next one is secondary, and not to be indulged in for the sake of an abstract completeness that betrays its next step by its usurpation of mental resources. For example, a moral ideologist has no business in speculating about utopian schemes of peace for the whole world until he is able to bring peace into small social units like a family, preferably his own. Ideological knowledge (i.e. justified belief, strictly speaking) must begin necessarily with the knowledge of where men are in order that it may inspire men morally to move where they ought to be; without knowledge of actual conditions there can be no real connection to the next step.

Justified belief, in an ideological world-view, is the heart of its moral creativity. Cognitively speaking, it must begin with such normative essentials as *agape,* reasonableness, or the highest commitments of civilized humanitarian values; without these it easily degenerates into a force of contention for 'who is right' rather than 'what is right.' It must be highly self-critical and reject any beliefs that do not possess the qualities of sincerity capable of making these beliefs an active way of life for any and all men.

Action, as an essential element in the conceptual framework of an ideological world-view, is based, not merely upon its own possibility or desirability, but upon the necessity of an ideological world-view to recognize that men must decide, the ideological implication of which is that the efficiency of our action is a moral question. On the basis of the necessity of decision, it is more important for an ideology to aid and create moral efficiency than it is for scientific discovery to be efficient, since the moral life has no chance to repeat the experiment.

The 'relations' or 'relatedness' necessary to the world-view of a moral ideology is primarily epistemological, concerning the proper cognitive interaction of the essentials of knowledge, justified belief, and action. In order to avoid the moral barrenness of intellectualism, knowing must have an active relation to justified belief and action; in order to avoid the immoral use of ideology (i.e. ideologism) , beliefs and values must justify themselves morally by an honest relation to knowledge and pragmatically by the ability to sustain consistent moral action; in order to avoid a perverted stupidity, action must be related to knowledge, and to avoid the unbalance of scientism, it must be related to the belief commitments (i.e. moral norms) of a civilized humanity.

Balance is basically a matter of moral integrity, the art of knowing what to do in the circumstances through care for men's deepest needs; the balance of how much thinking and how much doing can only be judged by what it does to preserve and advance the highest attainments of men. A good intellectual would not be contemplating when he should be actively defending the right to contemplate, nor would a good prophet be in action before he was clear on his goals and his commitment to them. For such balance simple sincerity does wonders.

The world-view of a moral ideology only attains a balanced relation of essentials through the clarity that can only result through a decisional commitment to be relevant to the deepest moral needs of men and nations. It must focus only in cognition and action relevant to its task, morality. It must eschew irrelevant intellectual curiosity as the "lust of the mind" and any useless action as the "lust of the flesh." Basic to the attainment of a balanced relation of essentials, in an ideological world-view capable of meeting the deepest needs of men and nations, is a morally and ideologically adequate concept of the nature of man.

The Element of the Nature of Man in the World-View of a Moral Ideology

A moral ideology must include in its world-view a conceptual approach to the nature of man which accurately comprehends the key human factors essential to man's moral change or betterment. Since any unrealistic view of man's nature will only result in excessive speculation and argument with little improvement in the conduct of men, it is necessary for a moral ideology to describe where man *is* before it can inspire him to change to what he ought to be. C. I. Lewis says,

> Without a bedrock of social mores, and clarity in social aims, the possibility of further progress could be prejudiced, and the quality of individual life could be sacrificed in some breathless attempt at readjustments too pervasive and too beset by personal frustration for the human framework to endure. Perhaps we near that juncture where it would be opportune to inaugurate a five-year plan for reflection and meditation upon this kind of fact.
>
> Certain it is that the time now approaches when, if even the presently acquired store of information and know-how were to become universally shared and commonly exploited among men, the major remaining problem would hardly be that of further conquest of the natural environment but instead that of human self-control and self-direction.
>
> Once more in history, the understanding which man most needs is self-conscious and self-critical understanding of himself. And this time it is beyond all doubt that the requirement is to understand himself as a social animal, if he wishes to control his further history. (54:42)

The Corrigible Present in the Nature of Man.—Human self-control and the control of man's further history is essentially an ideological task which must be taken step by step; the failure to stress this philosophically and to insist upon it pragmatically is a major cause in the moral failures of men and nations. This failure centers in the ignorance of men of their own particular moral condition, which allows their inflated opinions of themselves to cause them to take moral step number two, three, four, five, . . . or ten, before they have taken step number one. An adequate view of human nature must avoid speculative generalities about mankind that are resistant to being applied to the moral needs of particular men in the present. Paton says,

> There is too often a tendency—it is the mark of over-intellectualism—to regard the moral problem mainly as one of criticism, of praising and blaming others, and incidentally of praising and blaming our past selves or our past actions. We forget that there would be no moral problem at all if we did not have to live and act in a society. The primary ques-

79

tion of morality for a good man—the one that arises directly
in action—is not 'What ought you to do?' It is not 'What
ought you to have done?' It is not even 'What ought I
to have done?' The primary question is 'What ought I to
do now?' The other questions are derivative; and it is a mistake to tackle them first and then apply the results to the
pressing problem of my own duty here and now. (79:293)

The only corrigible part of man's nature is the "here and now," and
the only "here and now" that is corrigible must begin in particular
men, since corrigibility must deal with particular needs in intelligent sequence. Speculative generalities are of little use in curing
moral needs; a moral ideology requires a universal concept of the
nature of man which readily lends itself to translation into terms
of the "here and how" of particular men as a first link in the chain
to the universal moral needs of all men.

The concept 'adequate description' is more dynamic in a moral
ideology than it would be in a merely scientific framework; 'adequate' must honor scientific accuracy but still be free on the one
hand to exclude all that is not vital to human betterment and, on
the other hand, to include volitional elements essential in the moving of an accurate 'is' toward a justified 'ought.' Psychology and
related disciplines (23:14) are not presently adequate to do this,
since their concepts of adequate description are limited to scientific
objectivity. The description of man's nature in a moral ideology
requires qualities which are better thought of in terms of honesty
or sincerity. To point up the difference, it is enlightening to consider the added dynamic force found in sincere confession, over
and above mere objective admission of moral or spiritual wrong-
doing. The admission of a wrong act to a psychologist may be all
the objectivity the science of psychology requires; but when the
ideological concept of unity begets active decisions of moral reconciliation where the wrong-doer confesses his wrong act to the one
he had wronged, then a new level of objectivity occurs in the form
of reasonableness or sincerity. It is a form of cognition born only
through moral change.

Adequate description of man's nature is even less likely to
occur when the scientific degenerates into the scientistic. Helmut
Schoeck makes a good analysis in his claim that the "scientistic in-

terpretation of the study of man throws the scholarly grasp of human nature and its volitions open to ideological manipulations when least suspected" (Ap. 74). The way to avoid the gross mistakes of scientism, in comprehending the nature of man, is to consider the proper role that pre-scientific or extra-scientific factors must play in proper cooperation with the descriptive factors of science. It is often both instructive and necessary to take what may be considered an extra-scientific attitude in the approach of a moral ideology to the nature of man, where the ideological category of sincerity (purity of heart in religion) supersedes the scientific ideal of objectivity. The implication of this ideological sincerity for the moral ideologist is to show men their own natures in a way to minimize the gap between what they do and what they know to be right, i.e. how to be reasonable (Ap. 75).

Certain attitudes of moral sincerity must not be merely described but shared with those who are seeking to be men of good will; one such idea of sincerity, which seems to go beyond mere scientistic and even scientific objectivity, is the attitude of putting the benefit of the doubt in the right place. For example, in a scientific approach to one's own moral nature, it may make no difference in judging one's motives to test them from (1) the attitude of whether the particular act in question will not hurt anything, or from (2) the attitude of whether this act will do something specifically good; clarity on the difference in these two approaches, even from the same moral principle, gives the ideologists the creative edge over many "good people" who are never very clear on what their actions are good *for*. Unfortunately, the immoral ideologies have channeled much of recent history by means of the *dynamic* that this distinction gives; they have realized the inability of scientists in general to see this difference, and have capitalized on the vacuum the scientistic approach has created, and which the purely scientific approach as yet has found no effective way to correct.

The distinction between the two attitudes mentioned above, (1) morality on the basis of what will not hurt anything and (2) morality on the basis of what will do something specifically good, is a basic difference similar to Bergson's closed and open, i.e. static and dynamic, forms of morality. The moral life is as unlikely to be

81

creative in maintaining the first attitude as it is unlikely for an army to be victorious in a totally defensive war. The ideologist can usually tell a great deal about the moral nature of men by seeing which one of these attitudes dominates; to miss this part of the description of human nature is to miss the key to moral transformation in a great segment of mankind. It is the difference that results in a clear description of the passive versus the active attitudes of morality in men. For the ideologist there is something perverse about the idea that passive morality is sufficient (Ap. 76).

The moral description of the nature of a man and man in general has a necessary presupposition, if the description itself is to be within the sphere of moral sincerity. This presupposition is that the ideologist must begin a proper description of the character needs of other men by a sincere description of himself, if he is to be sincerely empirical. Ideology is a program to change things, and nothing is so resistant to moral change as the human will when those who prescribe change have not accepted and experienced change in the same moral area themselves. This is the point where mere theorizing and prescribing may find their most perverse expressions. The human will is more inclined to accept change by a sympathy of fellowship, where the ideologist takes the moral lead by sharing the experience of his own vital moral change with others. Nothing less than shared experience of moral change is ideologically sincere, because all the other prescriptive approaches have a tendency to degrade the man needing moral change by falsely exalting the moralist. The very assumption that human nature is reasonably uniform belies all moral methods that do not begin the process of moral change within the moralist himself. Empirically speaking, any man seeking to mediate moral change must have first experienced moral change; he must have already experienced his own need of change as much as he thinks he experiences such a need in others. In the realm of moral ideology, it is not important to describe one's theoretical moral level of attainment (this would be only speculative at best); it is, instead, more important to be clear on one's own willingness to live only by good will, reasonableness, and sincerity. Unfortunately, contemporary philosophical ethics have done little more than to mention these qualities without throwing much light upon them in their living contexts; hence their adequate description has been left to ideology.

It is extremely difficult for those who reject all ideology to understand its contribution to a study of the nature of man; this is the contribution of the idea that an adequate description of the moral life reveals unique priorities in the necessity of putting first things first. Often these priorities cannot be fully grasped on the basis of logical priority alone; one cannot make the claim that it is a logical priority to say, "if you want others to change, you ought to begin with changing yourself." It is even difficult to say that this statement implies a psychological priority, since in professional psychological counseling, this issue is seldom brought up on the basis of science, even though it may be treated more often on the basis of the psychologist's personal success as a counselor. To most contemporary philosophical ethics, the question of the priority of moral change within the ethicist as a necessary prerequisite to accurate moral description is usually considered to be about as relevant as the same issue would be to a mathematician. Nevertheless, within a moral ideology this issue is central because of the active nature of ideology in effecting an active program of change.

Elements Necessary to Morally Sound Ideological Efforts in the Change of Human Nature.—Once it has described man's moral condition adequately, an ideological account of the nature of man must accent man's moral advance, i.e. a change in human nature. Any successful efforts at moral creativity through human change must be based upon an overarching attitude about man's nature which implies: (1) the avoidance of unnecessary dogmatism, (2) a comprehension of the human will, and (3) the conservation of man's highest moral attainments. These attitudes will be considered in order.

In the moral realm unnecessary dogmatism must be avoided, and where dogmatism is relevant it must be used sparingly and intelligently. It becomes obnoxious particularly when an ethical theory is paraded as an established fact; this does not mean that men should not take a firm stand for their theoretical framework, but it does mean, particularly for ideology, that theories are at best a form of, more or less, justified belief.

A moral ideology would destroy its basic effectiveness if it afforded itself the luxury, common to much theology and philosophy, of going into endless arguments and speculations concerning the nature of man. On the one hand it must avoid the dogmatic approach of the notorious ideologies that simply insist that a certain race or class is the highest expression of human nature, and on the other hand it must avoid the attitude found in philosophical intellectualism (through its unawareness of the nature of the human will) which insists that ideological differences can be settled merely by an understanding of one another's philosophy. A moral ideology must avoid all dogmatism that is irrelevant to, or interferes with, the immediate improvement of concrete human nature.

Where the solutions of various immediate problems of men are essentially the same, unnecessary dogmatism may beget a perverse form of moral confusion. This type of argumentative dogmatism is frequently found, for example, among religionists who counterfeit volitional confusion for intellectual profundity, spending their time trying to complicate truth in order to avoid its moral demands. To be bound by such arguments as the depravity of man's nature, pro or con, can be morally perverse and ideologically stupid if the basic answer is the same. Whether the theological doctrine of human depravity is correct or not, it is likely that all men of good will would at least begin the first step with the same solution; this would be the willingness to change morally, in spite of how base or noble man is at present. The willingness to change toward what is right often must be created through some sort of motivation or inspiration, since no other moral steps can happen in actuality without willingness first. Any experienced ideologist knows that this is a major step requiring considerable intelligence and moral *dynamic* even if it seems theoretically trite. Willingness to change personally is ideologically prior to any point-of-view about the goal of mankind socially; nothing less constitutes commitment to good will or reasonableness.

Any dogmatism that displaces or overshadows this focusing of men on reasonableness is the enemy of all morally sound ideology. After all, the point-of-view is not so important, particularly if it is only a theory, when the improvement of the human will requires the same treatment from both points of view.

Since ideology must lay much of its moral ground work man

to man, it must avoid the dogmatism that comes from moral finger-pointing. In the moral realm there are few things as offensive to the human psyche as a moralist who demands others to change but has not pioneered the process of moral change within himself. This point needs no argument, but only the memory of the use of such hypocrisy upon ourselves personally. The man who is never perverse is a fiction. C. I. Lewis says, "human perversity is as perennial as the rationality it belies" (54:93). Even though all men do realize that this applies to them, it is difficult to begin with themselves. "Criticism is always harder to take than information, even when it is self-criticism" (54:94). But particularly if one has any program to change society, this is where he must begin.

The second point to consider in an ideological approach to changing human nature is to comprehend the nature of the human will, at least in its relation to those factors which create its most efficient moral response and growth (i.e. a vital relation between the elements on the left side of the diagram of Appendix 1 with those on the right).

An ideological approach points out the distinction between 'consistent' demand (for example, of Kant's 'duty') and 'total' demand. Consistent demand has little or no way of dealing with moral passivity, since the question is limited to *what* motive; it has no way of dealing with a morality that is consistent but mediocre. Those who are well acquainted with a moral ideology have made the statement,

> the will responds to total demands. It has peace only when there is singleness of purpose demanding total effort. Its basic need is to give everything for something great. (14:16)

In the moral life there must be the presupposition of consistency; to say that one will be consistent some of the time means absolutely nothing to morality, in spite of its possible significance for psychology. Even though being consistent is necessary, however, giving ourselves totally for what is right some of the time has more moral significance than the consistent giving of ourselves partially all of the time. One who has experienced the freedom and *dynamic* of total commitment at least once knows what he is betraying in himself when he becomes morally half-hearted. The man who has never responded to total singleness of moral purpose at any one time completely misses the dynamic dimension of morality, even though he may be fully consistent and ninety-nine percent committed. Even if he is consistent with his principles, it is his self-legislated one percent of compromise with total demand upon his will that destroys his moral *dynamic*. In the area of consistency, morality, like logic, cannot tolerate even one exception. The exception of one's right to break the moral law is not the issue here; it is moreover one's self-legislated "right" to be insensitive about the dynamic or creative factors in the moral life. Without creative and dynamic factors morality becomes abstract theorizing, or a push and pull affair with oneself and others. This highly creative dynamic factor is commitment to a moral form of self-legislated 'total demand' mentioned above in a vital relation with the consistency most ethical systems presuppose.

It is the element of total moral demand upon oneself in the corrigible present that takes the mind and will out of the energy sapping calculations and argumentations of proving who was right, and elevates the will into the non-calculating freedom to do what is right. Naive moral reasoning assumes that a one percent compromise in our moral living will beget only an equal percentage of confusion in our moral thinking. Mature moral reasoning about the nature of the will understands that there is no direct or fixed proportion of moral confusion to compromise. In a morally sensitive person a very small moral compromise may result in a near total crippling of his moral creativity; he is aware that his moral exception is self-given, and because it happens rarely, gives no moral assurance to the conscience that his standards exist at all once any exceptions are admitted for convenience. The conscience cannot tolerate exceptions to moral norms any more than the intellect can tolerate exceptions in the foundational concepts of logic; consequently it is not strange that the moral resembles the logical. C. I. Lewis says that "the root of logic itself lies in the fact of decision, and decision as constraint upon future attitude" (52:86) . Whereas moral understanding lies in decision for consistency, actual moral creativity lies in the decision of total demand upon oneself.

The self-given total demand, exhibited in some forms of moral reconciliation, is indicative of a moral "consistency" that logic does not demand but which logic may fully accept. This is the dimension of reconciliation on a total basis. Western moral philosophies are generally a bit unreal in their assumption that man's moral task is only to avoid moral wrong-doing. There has been a considerable neglect of major forms of right-doing about reconciling the moral wrongs that have always been directly confronting man since systematic thinking began. It is like a group of sailors sitting on the deck theorizing about how to avoid leaks in the hull of a ship that is already sinking, instead of thinking how to repair the holes already there. The practical issues of going about to repair the particular moral breaches in society are the job of the moralist; but the question of 'reconciliation's role' within moral philosophy is a philosophical issue. To miss this point is to neglect one of the most important factors in the normative approach to the nature of man. Only perfect men can afford to make reconciliation a point that is non-foundational.

A classic example of the response of the human will to "total demand" is the idea of 'total responsibility' for moral wrong-doing on the part of the offender. Those who have had much experience in trying to improve the nature of particular men, as well as man in general, know that reconciliation is one of the key issues that must be dealt with before men can move into the realm of creative morality. It is very much like the moral issue of the obligation to pay one's current debts before lavishing in unnecessary luxuries. A prominent trait of human nature is to pay back moral "debts" it has not incurred in order to avoid the moral debts it has incurred through moral wrong-doing; for example, it is much easier to say pleasant things about a person to compensate for our slander of his character than to make full restitution to the victim about our act of slander. Those who understand the nature of the will realize that in such cases the will has its own kind of "logic." A self-centered will is inclined to put the blame on its victim, particularly if the wrong-doing was mutual. A morally mature person has learned to take full responsibility for his failures; this means that his restitution does not depend upon what his opponent does, even if his opponent began the trouble and was responsible for the major part of the strained relationship. The mature moral man is more likely to heighten his own responsibility when others begin

87

to lower theirs. The question of who was mostly at fault is irrelevant to those whose wills have been matured by the self-given attitude of 'total demand' mentioned above; in this case it would be total demand in the line of responsibility for reconciliation over and above proving who was right. The mature moral will is usually marked by its willingness to begin to put things right even if it was the minor offender; it uses the kind of moral reasonableness that says, "if the other fellow was ten times as wrong as I was, then it is ten times easier for me to begin the process of reconciliation." This may not be logical to the selfish or the morally dogmatic, but it is the creative edge of a moral ideology.

In summary, moral reasonableness presupposes both a full measure of moral consistency, and total moral demand upon oneself; it is only by such decisions that a moral ideology can begin to approach the goal of the "new type of man." What the ethical philosopher calls reasonableness in philosophy is the new type of man in ideology; the new type of man is concrete reasonableness in the flesh. Where reason implies logical consistency, reasonableness implies a change, just as any act of doing does. In fact, 'reasonableness' means that one will do what he knows to be right on a totalistic as well as a consistent basis. The willingness to change for the better totalistically as well as consistently is a characteristic of the new type of man who embodies the ideological transformation of the human will.

The third point to consider in an ideological approach to the nature of man is the conservation and development of man's highest moral attainments; in this area the ideological approach must be firm and unwavering. It is the moral problem of being firm on the right issues but not the wrong ones, and this must be developed through a sincere study of man's moral history along with a careful consideration of principles. These two elements have too often been separated by intellectualists who neglect a proper relational balance of description and norms.

The conservation of the highest values is the mark of sincerity in the true liberal as well as the conservative of open mind and good will; it is a conservation of values which is above the pseudo-liberalism that amounts to no more than left-wing dogmatism, and it is also above the pseudo-conservatism that cleaves to the outmoded effects of good principles when the principles themselves have already led on to higher expressions. In fact, most of the higher values supersede the pseudo-issues of liberal versus conservative, since neither of these ideas has been developed clearly enough to match the highest moral norms with any high degree of consistency. Therefore, both the honest liberal and the honest conservative will seek to preserve the highest moral ideas and ideals. The question of liberal or conservative, right-wing or left-wing is irrelevant on this higher moral level, and to make this question basic is to begin from sub-moral principles which prejudice the issues from the beginning by betraying 'what is right' for the sake of arguing on the false premise of 'who is right.' Man's highest moral attainments are, in a sense, inclined to reach out beyond mere point-of-view toward the higher values and norms which are basically ideological (i.e. toward highly justified beliefs, demonstrable only upon the presupposition of moral good will and sincerity). Since these attainments require ideological factors that scientific facts do not require, their objectivity is a matter of reasonableness and not mere reason.

The highest value concepts are ideological because of their unprovability, but they are the only tools available to improve the welfare of humanity. The idea of 'respect for the human person' and the 'sanctity of life' were born as concepts of New Testament faith; they were re-discovered by the Reformation and given a higher factual status politically by men such as Roger Williams and Thomas Jefferson. The concepts of the American Revolution have been highly praised by men of every class and race; for example, the idea that 'all men are created equal' has been re-echoed around the world ever since. Nevertheless, this highly respected concept is distinctly ideological, and since 'equality' does not happen automatically it presupposes a considerable amount of directed moral change within the societies that realize this principle through experience. It is the cutting edge of the American and similar legal systems, and as such it is used as a tool and weapon against those who would degrade the human personality to their own advantage. 'Equality' is an ideological tool which has demonstrated its own use in a fully democratic and morally respectable way, giving the ground work for men to discover and to cooperate in a type of moral creativity which goes out beyond selfishness. Nevertheless there must be other ideological concepts related to that of equality in order to obtain the most highly creative results. These will be discussed later under the heading "The Dynamic Factors of a Moral Ideology" in chapter 6.

These efforts to conserve man's highest moral attainments have been reaffirmed in such documents as the Four Freedoms, in 1941, and the Universal Declaration of Human Rights, which was adopted and proclaimed by the General Assembly of the United Nations in 1948 (15:21, 22). They all presuppose the dignity of man and the worth of the individual; consequently a moral ideology must seek to preserve and even foster these ideas to their highest development. The existence of ideologies in the world, attempting to destroy these moral ideals, does not change the ideological status of these ideals themselves; on the contrary, it shows the relevance of these libertarian principles in the ideological arena. Furthermore, it does not imply that a moral ideology itself cannot be one of the best forms of defense for these ideals. After all, it is difficult to defend such concepts solely on the basis of scientific objectivity. 'The worth of the individual' finds its objectivity only in the form of good will between men; it is an objectivity which is different from the objective facts of science which must be admitted "in spite of" our wills. For this reason a moral ideology is a definite means of preserving these ideals, because it is designed to deal with the human will in proper relation to the objective facts of science.

In summary, the present issue of the conservation of man's highest moral attainments is in great measure ideological, although it is one demanding that an ideology realize its own limitations. This ideological 'humility' implies: (1) strict deference to universal moral norms, (2) the refusal to parade beliefs as knowledge in order to justify the wrong use of force or to violate man's right to choose for himself, (3) the repudiation of abstract generalities which betray the moral reasonableness and good will of dealing with first things first.

The Element of a Systematic Methodology

A methodology, a synthesis of doing and knowing, is the third essential of a moral ideology, which completes the relational triangle composed of a *dynamic,* a world-view, and a methodology (Ap. 1). Although it is not as distinctly a philosophical element as the world-view, a well-developed methodology is absolutely necessary if an ideology is to attain the high degree of balance essential to pragmatic effectiveness.

The Methodology of an Ideology and Science.—The methodology is the element of an ideology that is most closely related to science; science cannot give values, but it can give aid and clarification on many of the most direct and systematic ways to attain these values. An ideology would even fail the moral as well as the pragmatic test if it did not seek to alleviate human moral need in the most direct and efficient way possible.

The Methodology of an Ideology and Moral Norms.—The major question in a moral ideology concerns keeping the methodology or plan of action within the limits of the highest moral norms, particularly since it is in this area that some major ideologies have become immoral, in spite of their allegedly noble aims. These norms must function as stabilizing elements of the ideology in its methodological plan of action, hence the philosophical problem at stake is that the plan of action of an ideology ought to be submitted completely to the criticism of moral norms. An equally important philosophical problem for a moral ideology is that it must attain the proper dynamic level as a highly effective plan of action; for example, this plan must meet the pragmatic test of being able to impel the world-view of the ideology into actuality. Since an ideological plan of action must be effective as well as moral, ideology reveals its close kinship, or even identity, with certain forms of pragmatic philosophy.

The Methodology Is Necessitated by the Unavoidability of Decision.—The most respectable form of pragmatism to date is the conceptualistic pragmatism of C. I. Lewis, whose philosophy can contribute much to ideology in the way of philosophically rigorous stabilizing factors without petrifying the dynamic side of ideology. Lewis himself, as far as I know, does not necessarily advocate the ideological approach to social problems, but he does show the necessity of beliefs and decision in a way which reveals his understanding of basic ideological issues (52:38, 86). Philosophical systems that do not understand "that to decide is unavoidable" (52: 86) also fail to understand that the methodological 'plan of action' is necessitated by the unavoidability of decision. The very necessity of some decision leaves only the choice of being more or less reasonable and intelligent in causing our decisions to lead coherently toward effecting a moral world-view. Consequently, if one realizes the unavoidability of decision concerning the actuation of a moral world-view, then it cannot have 'world' significance outside of some systematic or consistent means to reach such a broad area; this is, by any name one chooses to call it, a methodology.

Even though the methodological plan of action is the scientific or technological side of an ideology, it is more like the technique of a painter or violinist, because the plan has to be "artistically" *dynamic* as well as technically competent. Christianity has even gone so far as to express this plan in terms of a Person, the person of Christ (Eph. 1: 9, 10; Col. 1:27—29). Yet even on this mystical level the step by step details must be worked out in a technically competent way. The mark of moral competence, as well as technical and scientific competence, must reveal itself through the justified beliefs of an ideology which cause its adherents to put 'first things first' and to maintain a balanced relation of essentials in their thinking and actions. It will be sufficient here to say that 'first things first' will be an attitude of the 'sanctity of the person' on the moral level, and an attitude that 'we must change individual men in order to change society' on the pragmatic level.

Essentially the plan of action of an ideology is a philosophical question in the same sense that action is a subject of moral philosophy. Because decisions cannot be avoided, it is only reasonable to make them with as much foresight and coherence as possible. In essence this is a philosophical commitment to a plan of action over and above mere action (Ap. 77).

The Methodological Plan of Action as a Moral Laboratory.— It is a basic philosophical premise of this inquiry that acting upon justified belief is as necessary as acting upon empirical knowledge. The point at issue in this section is that methodological action is almost as significant for philosophy as it is for ideology. Moral philosophy itself could be more empirically sound and less scholastic if it were willing to use a plan of action as a moral laboratory (chapter 6) ; the only level of experimental reality it is necessary to insist upon in this connection is that the philosopher himself should comprehend some moral plan of action through personal experience, since anything less would be prejudice. The role of a moral ideology is to work this out systematically on a social scale.

CHAPTER 5

THE STABILIZING FACTORS OF A
MORAL IDEOLOGY

There are at least three major stabilizing factors of the moral life which in combination are best exemplified in moral ideology or its philosophical equivalent. The first is conscience, which stabilizes moral consistency in consequence of the inner demand of principles that go beyond the exigencies of the moment or particular situation. The second is the role of stabilizing norms, in the form of commitment to moral (not metaphysical) absolutes; among these is reasonableness, an absolute which stabilizes the decisive relating of principles to action. The third is the stabilizing factor of the balanced language, which implies a proper relation of the languages of intellect and will; this prevents an ethical unbalance that results from the domination of factors which either, on the one hand, enlighten the intellect but fail to mobilize the will, or, on the other hand, mobilize the will without proper normative enlightenment of the intellect.

The first and third of these stabilizing factors may seem to resemble or even be identified with the dynamic elements of the moral life, and in comparison to many static systems they are dynamic. Nevertheless, in comparison to the force-giving dynamics of the next chapter, these elements function to create a stability involving progress, analogous to the situation of an airplane in flight which is stabilized by the rudder and control surfaces against capricious maneuvers.

The Fact of Conscience as a
Stabilizing Element

Conscience, the Basic Assumption of Moral Stability.—Conscience, as a cognitive reality, must be assumed as the basic precondition of moral stability, just as the uniformity of nature must be assumed as the basic precondition of scientific stability (Ap. 78). There is a definite knowledge factor in conscience. In the functioning of conscience, one can do no better than to believe reasonably or assume the validity of its highest demands, but one may know in his conscience when he betrays the moral norms conscience must believe or assume; the knowledge factor centers in the knowledge of one's integrity in particular situations. He must "know" by assuming the validity of the highest common aims of society, and as C. I. Lewis concludes,

> . . . we still have no alternative but to conduct ourselves on the *assumption* [my italics] of their validity and the possibility of their furtherance. Otherwise the common vocation of man would lack significance. (54:110)

Without the primacy of the moral principle there are no valid grounds for a criterion of social improvement (54:109).

Kant regarded conscience to be the basic fact of human experience. In Beck's description of Kant's position, "Obligation is characterized by subjective necessity, the objective counterpart of which is moral law" (39:32). It was on the premise of assuming that conscience was the basic reality, implying the centrality of practical action, that Kant opened the way for ideological philosophies. All of the outstanding ideologies tend to give conscience a foundational role. The distortion of conscience, by ideologies like Nazism and Marxism-Leninism, for the purpose of stabilizing their ideological goals as some sort of fact, does not refute its important role. They have used the conscience to reinforce a type of "axiological ought" (94:430) that informs the adherents of the ideologies mentioned above what values they ought to pursue and how they ought to be pursued.

A moral ideology on the other hand allows conscience to stabilize itself on a critical basis where conscience normatively criticizes the ideological goals, and particularly its means or plans of action. The moral ought in certain forms may not directly pertain to means or ends, but conscience will reveal, if given a free chance, whether the means and ends of an ideology can be subsumed under the moral ought. For example, every man is under obligation as a member of the human race to reject the claim that one race

96

(Nazism) or one class (Marxism) shall globally rule. The world leaders who have rejected their full obligation as members of the *human* race have put themselves in moral jeopardy of becoming international criminals. These men have not generally denied the fact of conscience, they have merely reduced it to a tool of their own devices. But conscience must be more than just a fact of the moral life; it must be the central fact, especially for ideology. Yet conscience must be trained and refined; this is the task of moral standards or norms.

Although conscience is recognized by many thinkers as a fact, this does not necessarily imply that they see its true nature. In the same sense, no one doubts man as a fact, but this does not imply any accurate account of his nature, particularly the nature of what he ought to be.

Those who have de-emphasized the role of will and belief in the human psyche usually incline towards a reductionistic view of conscience. The conscience is our most significant form of belief involving a balanced and coherent relationship of will and intellect (Ap. 79) ; the only way to cognize the nature of conscience is to begin by accepting the highest dictates of one's own conscience by a decision of the will. This practice is not as common as one might think in the higher levels of conscience, since these higher demands involve considerable belief and are therefore most easily rationalized away. Even if one accepts conscience as a fact, the giving of proper scope to it is a matter of belief and good will tested by knowledge and intelligence. In conscience, the knowledge components are the stabilizing but negative factors; the positive or creative factors are beliefs. It is on the belief edge that the human conscience advances. The difference between the civilized and the primitive conscience is that the civilized conscience perceives the need of its own consistent advance in relation to some kind of law or norm (Ap. 80) .

The mark of the mature conscience is the inner demand of impartial concern for the welfare of other human beings (Ap. 81) ; it is a trend away from self-centeredness toward a dignified form of voluntary cooperation.

The Need of Action and Decision in Stabilizing Conscience.— The power of conscience consists in the reality that its valid dictates are not mere fabrications of isolated minds (Ap. 82) ; if such were the case, the conscience would grow weaker with time. Hocking says,

> Mental traits that come down to us from antiquity grow weaker as we recede from the source, whereas conscience, like the aesthetic sense, grows more sensitive, and gives rise from time to time to men of moral genius, who develop new ethical ideas. There is no doubt a fund of inherited feeling which attends certain moral requirements which are deep rooted in the race, such as the revulsion against murder, unchastity, and perhaps theft. But conscience itself moves ahead of ancestral requirements, and hence cannot be explained away as a mere biological inheritance. (32:97)

Hocking also points out that as conscience grows more sensitive, it reaches the level of genius in some people such as Socrates where it grows most active;

> Thus in the career of Socrates, we have a literary record of the work of conscience—personified as his "daemon"—in guiding his decisions at critical junctures. In him, conscience appeared as an unanalyzed sense of wrongness warning him away from certain courses of action which he was inclined to adopt. These actions were incongruous with some inner standard of whose nature he was hardly aware. That inner standard, we may suppose, is simply the persistent mystical sense of unity with the Real; and conscience is the intuitive recognition that a proposed course of action is, or is not, consistent with that unity. (32:272)

All conscience is based upon some element of unity; the question of a well-developed conscience is the extensiveness of that unity on both a personal and social level. Theoretical unity is necessary; however, above all other philosophical considerations, the subject of conscience can least afford to stop at mere theoretical unity. The subject of conscience can only avoid an unrealistic reductionism by finding a relational unity of consistent theory and action. As in Hocking's words quoted above, "conscience is the intuitive recognition that a proposed course of action is, or is not, consistent with that unity." Now this "course of action" refers to action in general of this or that type and is theoretical as such; but conscience needs to be more than theoretical if it is to remain conscience and not a mere conceptualizing about right and wrong. Conscience must decide. First it must make a decision to be objective about the Real. It is true, of course, that,

> conscience is variable; for conscience would be clear only as the sense of unity within the Real is strong, and this sense might require renewal from time to time by deliberate acts of attention. (32:272)

It is at this point of deliberate renewal that decisions of good will enter, over and above theoretical unity.

Decision is an absolute necessity in the development of conscience; although the intellect may attain marked development solely on the descriptive plane, the conscience requires the definite relating of facts to norms through decision. In matters of conscience, the moral agent has only one channel of firsthand information; this is the awareness that he has decided to be true to his own highest norms, a unique form of knowledge that arises in the will and is stabilized by the will.

The Relation of Conscience to Ideology.—The relationship of conscience to ideology is the same relationship conscience possesses to any normative social philosophy. The ideologies are usually more coherent in their plan of action than are social philosophies, and thus give the human decision procedure a more empirical basis upon which conscience may be tested more thoroughly concerning the validity of its claim to unity with the Real (which Hocking mentions in the last quotation above).

Ideology is capable, through its relational approach (Ap. 1), of testing and developing conscience in a non-atomic fashion that only the most developed religions can match. The religions that have developed conscience to a high level in various areas usually include their own highly developed ideology, or an equivalently rational and dynamic approach.

Both science and philosophy have aided conscience by clarifying the nature of knowledge. But even though knowledge is basic to many issues, there are many issues in which conscience must proceed upon belief. Ideology is basically mobilized belief, using knowledge as a stabilizing factor. The immoral ideologies force their beliefs upon humanity as if these beliefs were knowledge, thus twisting conscience to their own devices. A moral ideology must mobilize belief on a social scale in such a way that its leading edge is conscience guided by norms and not by mere point-of-view. It is on this highly empirical level of social action that conscience obtains a new sensitivity which mere abstract thinking cannot produce. In the relational approach (Ap. 1) to conscience, on the one hand, the coherence of conscience with facts and logic is revealed essentially through thinking or the intellect; on the other hand, the sensitivity of the conscience is developed through action or decision. Highly developed or well-thought-out social action, resulting from our beliefs of conscience, approximates a form of ideology.

It is currently impossible for an earnest and alert mind to overlook the great influence that the ideologies have exercised, pro and con, upon the conscience of contemporary man. One cannot escape the current problem that many of the most important issues of conscience have been precipitated by the manner in which ideologies have treated human conscience. Human conscience does not develop in a vacuum; since the beginning of the 19th century ideological philosophies and ideologies (for example, democracy, Marxism, evangelicalism) have had more influence in shaping conscience on a large scale than non-ideological approaches because of their definite, morally active world-views. On the negative side, the quasi-ideology of scientism has had a considerable deadening effect upon human conscience when its beliefs have been accepted as facts. This is similarly true of race and class-centered ideologies, which have sought to destroy whole areas of conscience and twist what is left toward their own ideological goals. Hence, a moral ideology must treat conscience as *a priori* to its own goals, even though conscience will likely be benefited by this ideology *a posteriori;* that is, conscience must judge ideology morally even though conscience may gain experiential sharpness through ideological activity.

The Contribution of Ideology to Conscience.—Conscience, tested by standards, must judge all ideology; only in this way can there be a truly moral ideology. On the other hand, conscience is heightened and made more sensitive in an ideological context, over and above a mere atomic and analytical context. It is here that the philosophical point becomes manifest, that collective, coherent, dynamic conscience is more than the sum of its individual parts.

On the basis of collective unity the conscience which is centered in the idea that "all men are created equal" may pass from a static equality-centered form into the higher, dynamic form of the *agape*-centered type (Ap. 83). The latter form of conscience must use the ideal of equality as its negative test, but move beyond it. The democratic, equality-centered conscience can be egocentrically individualistic whereas the *agape*-centered conscience cannot.

The Marxist-Leninist ideology maintains that its greatest form of ideological advantage over democratically minded people is the latter's moral blindness to the role of opportunism, one of the chief ideological tools the totalitarians use to compromise their enemies (Ap. 84) (84:150, 154, 156, 174, 192, 267, 299). The equality-centered, democratic conscience has had to date very little moral cure for opportunism, giving Mao Tse-tung the ideological occasion to say that opportunism will be the Marxist-Leninists' major tool in destroying the democracies and hence the democratic conscience (84:174). Consequently, the only sensible moral defense against the pernicious manipulations of conscience by immoral ideologies is to possess in the conscience a volitional sensitivity greater than that of the totalitarians, which relates to and supplements the more obvious philosophical necessity of the logical unity of conscience. It requires, in fact, a volitional sensitivity that would go beyond the limited "logical unity" of ethical systems based upon egoism or any form of reductionistic naturalism.

If the logical unity of the democratic conscience is based upon a fragmentary concept of the nature of the person (which is too often the case), then this produces a reductionistic "unity" of conscience which is gained at the expense of moral breadth. Those who possess a fragmentary concept of the moral will, and hence of their own moral failures, are easy targets for totalitarian ideologists who channel attitudes like opportunism to work against its possessors. For example, it is not that Marxist-Leninists are not themselves victims of their own opportunism, but that they know how to utilize the blindness of a conscience which has been limited and insensitized by opportunism (Ap. 84). Once the totalitarian ideologist discovers these weak points, he is often able to manipulate the wills of both individuals and groups to his own advantage by means of their ambition to gain positions of "moral" and political prominence without proper regard for principle.

The ideologists do know much about the human will, and could teach most intellectualists something valuable on the subject. The widespread intellectualistic aversion to will is not the result of scientific objectivity, but of the intellectualist's own will to be obscurantistic on the subject. It is at this point that intellectualists, in their avoidance of will, throw themselves open to the manipulations of immoral ideologists (84:268, 299). Those who do not understand the human will very seldom understand the subtle distinction between opportunism and the virtues which it counterfeits; it is in this area that well-meaning individuals are used by immoral ideologists, not because they lack conscience, but because they are ignorant of the ideological use of conscience and have little or faulty understanding of the nature of the human will in its collective form, i.e. ideological will (84:166, 171, 174, 177, 202, 266).

Ideology is the unity of will in a universal (or, at least, extensive) social field of active decision; hence any avoidance of decision to recognize such currently crucial social facts as the ideologies will have its deadening effect upon the conscience, and also result in playing the game of the immoral ideologies by default. The only alternative, to allowing one's conscience to be insensitized through neglect of such crucial facts as the ideologies, is systematically to develop conscience to include an active world-view that deals with the immoral ideologies which would subvert conscience; in effect this highly developed conscience implies both a moral ideology and a moral philosophy capable of a vital relationship to the ideological needs and challenges of the times. On the one hand, a moral ideology maximizes and stabilizes this relational enlargement of conscience beyond the bounds of a purely intellectualistic view of man's nature, in a manner that gives it a much stronger imperative in its over-all world-view. On the other hand, conscience, as long as it refuses to be the tool of ideology, calls ideology to account for itself, giving ideology a stability of motive which is supra-philosophical as well as philosophical.

THE STABILIZING FACTORS OF A MORAL IDEOLOGY

Absolute Norms as a Stabilizing Element

The conscience is a fact; but its growth and maturity have a reciprocal dependence, more or less, upon other facts. One of these is the fact of reasonable decision (to be discussed in chapter 6 under "The Dynamic Factors of a Moral Ideology") ; another is the fact of moral values and goals (not to be confused with theories about them) ; still another is the stabilizing factor of moral norms, now to be discussed.

Stabilizing Norms Must Be Absolute.—Without the actual element of stabilizing norms, conscience loses its necessary relation to reason; at this point all ideologies need to exercise ultimate care, for it is only on the basis of moral norms that their great dynamic forces can be channeled into meeting the needs of mankind. Without the stability of moral norms, the ideologies fail to meet men's deepest needs or, even worse, exploit men's weaknesses. The point is that moral standards have to be absolute if men want to avoid ideological manipulation of their consciences, either by their own passions or by the *dynamics* of ideologies that have no objective moral standards.

Only as moral standards remain firm against wilful capriciousness can they be a common social norm. They must be absolute, moreover, in the sense that they are accepted as absolutely binding and inspire commitment. This involves no unnecessary metaphysical dogmas; it merely requires that the individual accept them personally as ultimate norms which he hopes others will share, and who, at the same time, remains sufficiently open of mind to invite the further enlightenment by those who may have more authentic targets or standards. For Christians this ultimate is love (*agape*), identified with commitment to a Person or to persons, but without a complex of necessary metaphysical associations. Commitment is the essential principle: without it moral norms may be intellectually stimulating, but they have little relevance to man as a social being. Moral commitments are not mere intellectual games or even experiments; they are the stabilizing factors of a reasonable living where man has no second chance to repeat his moral acts. Hence their stability must be maximum without becoming an excuse for petrification.

The Justification of Moral Absolutes.—It is not possible to prove an absolute standard (p. 59) (this is not an ontological absolute which is infallibly changeless but an unreservedly accepted standard or 'practical absolute' which is necessary to sustain moral commitment) (Ap. 85) except to show that a 'relative standard' is a contradiction in terms (Ap. 86), especially on the volitional level. They may be effectively demonstrated to men of good will, however, not by ordinary proof as much as by our commitment to them and our decision to abide by them (94:432). For that matter, neither can we prove ultimates in any field of experience; moral standards must be apprehended without proof (94:390). Who but a perverse person needs "proof" of our obligation to good will or moral sensivity? H. J. Paton makes a relevant comment on this point:

> In actual practice complete moral scepticism is very rare. There are plenty of bad men willing to exempt themselves from all moral obligations, but they are not willing to extend this exemption to their neighbours, and then they begin to seem funny as well as immoral. They can see clearly enough that violence or treachery to themselves is an intolerable wrong —"you can't do this to me". Even Hitler appeared to be morally shocked at any fancied injustice done to his country. If we could find a genuinely amoral man—amoral not in some respects but in all—there would be nothing to do about him. He would just not be human. (79:292)

Public acceptance of a moral absolute is a way of announcing commitment to a stable moral order; and for this reason moral principles make no sense without the assumption that they are universally valid (94:425).

Absolute standards are not proved to be abstract or impossible because men may not accept them or put them into practice; they are moreover negative (Ap. 87) or quasi-negative elements that channel the more positive dynamic elements toward final goals.

The Respective Roles of Absolutism and Relativism.—From the point of view of a broad humanism, if not from a position of personalistic theism, Garnett seems to be correct in his claim that relativism does not come into contradiction when it stays within the realm of the nature of the 'good,' although the nature of the 'right' must be absolute (Ap. 88) . Relativism of values (excluding such values as truth or a personal relationship to God) is a justifiable point of view since everything less than God which man may value will likely be superseded by something higher. Man is bound to an absolute only in the sense that out of a choice of values, even though they evolve and change, he must choose what he honestly believes to be the highest.

The concept of fixed or absolute moral standards, in other words, must be seen from two aspects; that of the intellect and that of the will. From the point of view of the intellect, or the logical point of view, only an absolute standard can avoid being a contradiction in terms (Ap. 86) . Thus the very word 'STANDard' implies fixedness without exception, at least to a specific context in such a way as to exclude capriciousness of the moral will. From the point of view of the will, the idea of an absolute standard is understood in terms of a non-reversible decision to accept certain moral principles (Ap. 86) . These principles must be universal and formal because otherwise extensive good will might shortly come into conflict with itself. These principles moreover must not bend with the will; if they did, the situation would emerge in which, instead of the will being committed to principles, the principles would be "committed" to the will. This twist is the root of the major part of the immoral and unstable uses of the dynamic ideological forces.

Moral Principles and Moral Rules.—H. J. Paton has given one of the best insights into the nature of moral principles and their need of being absolute (Ap. 89) . He distinguishes between (1) moral principles, and (2) moral laws or rules. Moral laws or rules are only singular applications of the moral principles and are relative to the situation; but they are still absolute in that they hold for all men in like circumstances, and never depend merely upon our likings or dislikings. In any case, even though one's judgments about a particular situation are fallible (and true humility must be based on this realization) , he must "act as if" his judgments are binding; otherwise he might betray moral principles altogether.

Moral principles reveal their full meaning only as they are related to a whole system of rights and duties; breadth and depth

of moral insight can be gained "only in action" where the relationship of moral philosophy to ideology must be recognized, for only
within an ideological framework can one experience certain major
history-forming types of united action; there is no way to put
isolated moral experience on this plane of experience. Being sensitive in the smaller spheres of ordinary social relations does not ex-
pand our moral experience to an ideological level of adequacy,
even though the ideological level presupposes competence in the
smaller spheres.

*A Moral Ideology Demonstrates the Need of Commitment to
Principles.*—In dealing with the problems that alien (and even our
own) ideologies create, only a firm commitment to principles in
the form of absolute standards can give proper stability; in other
words, it takes the stability of an absolute standard (p. 59) to
channel the dynamic elements of some of our modern ideologies.
Nevertheless, between the dynamic factors of an ideology and the
stabilizing factors of absolute norms, the influence is reciprocal.
For example, even though moral principles must stand on their
own merit in order to channel and judge ideology, there also can
be a much clearer deduction of adequate moral rules from these
principles if the principles themselves stand in some sort of empirical or pragmatic relation to an ideology. In the face of actual
moral need, the ideology gives stability and breadth to our felt-
need of principles, and consequently to a faith that leads us to
commit ourselves to these principles.

There is a difference between principles as known, and a belief
in the principles one knows. Often only an ideological experience,
or its religious equivalent, can impress the moral agent with the
need of a sensitive commitment to these principles on both the
personal (active) and universal (theoretical) levels. It is here that
the philosophical point is to be made, that even if principles do
furnish their own sanctions, such sanctions may not be adequate
to compete with the dynamic forces of an ideological age, for an
ethical sanction does not necessarily provide dynamic sufficient to
compete successfully with immoral dynamic ideologies for the
minds of men. Principles that do not exist in the minds of men as
commitments lack reality and hence practical absoluteness.

Principles are the stabilizing factors of morality, and particularly of moral ideology. Nevertheless, the relational world-view that only a moral ideology can give stabilizes the conviction of the need of principles within the volitional side of man's being. Many thinkers have never seen the reciprocal role a moral ideology can play because they have never thought what a moral ideology would be if it did exist. Nothing tests the validity of principles over and above their logical consistency so well as acting upon them; furthermore, nothing tests universal principles so well as honest and intelligent action on a scale as universal as is presently possible. Such united action, even if it is given other names, is still ideology if it goes beyond the descriptive into the prescriptive element of universal human need; the cognitive framework is a dynamic moral philosophy. Only the united directing of human will on a grand scale, in the form of the free commitment to universal responsibilities and goals, will have any chance of maturing the will on a grand scale. Those who think human will is mature in general need another look at it (60:118, 122, 125, 132).

Hence the conclusion to be drawn from this is that the comprehension of moral principles in the intellect alone is inadequate; moral principles must be related to action. As C. I. Lewis points out,

> Any principle which could be basic for morals must be highly general and abstract. But that to which it must finally be applied will be some concrete situation in which deliberate decision is called for; an act to be determined under particular conditions which will affect what follows from it and—in the peculiarly moral type of situation—will involve others than the doer in the effects of it. (54:96)

There is at present nothing so able to stabilize the reciprocal relationship of moral principles to action as a moral ideology.

The Balanced Language of a Moral Ideology as a Stabilizing Element

The language of a moral ideology appeals to the will for consistency just as the language of academic philosophy appeals to the intellect for consistency; however, this does not imply that ideology does not appeal to the intellect as well as to the will. The will is best engaged by speaking the language of the will, and it must be stabilized by the language that coordinates the will with the intellect according to moral principles that are capable of being applied with equal facility to both will and intellect. It is in the area of this needed stability, brought through coordination of the active and the conceptual, that intellectualism and its derivatives have failed contemporary man's moral needs. This failure is inevitable as long as the moral problem is confined within the intellectualistic orbit; only a moral ideology or its equivalent can restabilize the needed active balance and only a dynamic moral philosophy can restabilize it conceptually.

Will Has Its Own Kind of Relational Consistency.—Moral thinkers ought not to be prejudiced on principle against ideologies simply because some ideologies are dominated by uncritical belief and will. It is the *moral* ideology that must find a balance of these factors in the light of empirical circumstances according to universal moral norms. To recommend that the proportion of each always be equal would be to prejudice the particular situation. Some cases require a predominance of the intellect, particularly when the question is one of weighing facts already present; in these cases language should be as epistemologically exact and consistent as possible. Other cases require accent on will where the only choice is between faiths, as in the situation of Jefferson's belief that religious liberty would lead to order rather than the anarchy his opponents predicted. Since his was a pilot venture, his will in the form of well-reasoned belief had to predominate in his ideology of freedom (Ap. 90). In the Declaration of Independence, again, Jefferson made a profound use of an amazingly balanced language of will-belief-intellect, without which it would have been inadequate as a revolutionary document.

There is, then, a consistency of the will that the language of moral intellectualism does not fully reveal, and this is exhibited in the language of a moral ideology. The intellectualistic error is due to its presupposition that because the methodologies of mathematics and similar disciplines help to clarify some phases, they are adequate to cover all phases of moral philosophy. Moral intellectualism is too often inclined to apply certain mathematically oriented methodologies to moral philosophy that are out of date even for mathematics. On this point C. I. Lewis observes that,

> It has been demonstrated, with a degree of precision and finality seldom attained, that the certitude of mathematics results from its purely analytic character and its independence of any necessary connection with empirical fact. Its first premises are neither those self-evident truths of reason which inspired the continental rationalists to imitate the geometric method nor the principles of intuitive construction which, for Kant, assured a basis of application to all possible experience; they are not even empirical generalizations, as Mill and other empiricists have thought. Rather, they are definitions and postulates which exhibit abstract concepts more or less arbitrarily chosen for the purposes of the system in question. Intrinsic connection with experience is tenuous or lacking. (53:vii, viii)

Moral philosophy cannot exist without this intrinsic connection with experience.

Although in disciplines which are not purely formal intellectualists frequently make the mistake of positing the abstraction of "pure" intellect (Ap. 91), a properly relational moral philosophy (Ap. 1) must avoid the correspondingly opposite mistake of positing a "pure" will. When thinking gets beyond the formal disciplines, or even behind them to their postulates, the will in the form of belief is present by necessity (Ap. 92). It is also present when the formal system is applied to cases of fact or to empirical matters; at this point theory has a necessary relation to decision (54:96).

The Language of a Moral Ideology and Well-Reasoned Belief.— The language of a moral ideology, marked by its inclusive recognition of the necessary role of will, reveals its respect for well-reasoned belief in the form of absolute standards, which serve as stabilizing elements. It speaks in a way that avoids the confusing of these stabilizing elements with its dynamic elements.

The language of the will is not anti-intellectual unless the user seeks to pervert the will; but the language of philosophical analysts has often omitted the specific type of language that the will needs in order to be inspired to want to be reasonable. This is the language of well-reasoned belief, and many have caused their own moral poverty by avoiding it. It is often necessary to speak of moral principles on a volitional level as well as a conceptual level; each level of language stabilizes the other. The conceptual level of language brings stability through clarity; the volitional level brings stability by keeping moral principles relevant to this world and to specific men, and by adding clarity and force to the reality of our commitment, or lack of it, to moral principles. The volitional level of language may add stability to principles in much the same way that a laboratory adds stability to scientific theorizing. Even if one considers this the minor premise of stability, it is a necessary premise. Essentially the language of a moral ideology is like that of any good ethical system, but it has the added factor of giving well-reasoned belief a more prominent role without relegating it to the limbo of emotion (Ap. 93). The recognition or use of this language also helps to reveal the volitional aspect of thought generally, which has been overlooked by philosophers who have been led to mistake beliefs for knowledge because of their linguistic practice of euphemizing their own beliefs.

The Language of the Will Used as a Stabilizing Element Begets the Necessity of Knowing the Characteristics of the Will.—In order to employ effectively the language of the will, certain distorting tendencies of the will must be recognized. One of these is a complicating of simple moral issues in order to avoid making a decision. This is generally called 'rationalization,' which amounts to perverting our moral norms and beliefs for the sake of some secret hope. The mature moral person can see that what is volitionally difficult may be intellectually simple (Ap. 94). For example, it may be volitionally difficult to return stolen property to its owner but this does not constitute intellectual complications. The intellectual complications usually emerge in such issues when, to our friends and to ourselves, we dishonestly seek to justify the wrong act to the one we have wronged.

Conversely, what is intellectually complicated may be morally simple. It is often intellectually difficult to be objective in a given situation; but the decision to abide by the standard of objectivity may be simple for the man who has no hidden motives in his inquiry.

110

It often happens that the purely intellectualistic approach to moral principles will incapacitate them as a basis for the deduction of rules which are pragmatically adequate for extensive action. Although all principles must pass the test of logical unity, this by itself does not make them relevant to the moral life; Bentham's principle of happiness, for example, is still sub-moral with or without logical unity. A purely rationalistic approach cannot intelligently speak the language of the will for the very reason that it has concealed from itself its own use of will in the choosing of its purely intellectualistic categories, and the reason theoreticians should know the language of the will is because they have a will themselves that may sneak into their own calculations at unexpected times. If will is not clearly recognized in all its phases, it is likely to beget an intellectualism which will become a dangerous but inadequate ideology, like scientism or theological institutionalism.

The great religions have within them, more or less, the capability of speaking to the volitional element in humanity; in fact, this is the way they began; the intellectualizing came later. Even the great moral principles that they inspired did not happen in a volitional vacuum; for example, the central moral principle of Christianity is decisive love, or more specifically *agape* (Ap. 95).

The principle of love, however, needs the quasi-negative test of its own moral implications such as honesty, purity, and unselfishness. These stabilize the actuality of the principle of love by forbidding the principle to exist within a morally false realm of abstraction. It is here that moral principles must differ from principles like those of mathematics which can tolerate abstraction. Moral principles, even if they are formal, cannot be abstract in the sense that they imply only a string of abstractions (Ap. 96). Love itself, if genuine, is a very concrete thing which tests itself by moral principles, like integrity and purity, that are general enough to be variously applied to changing situations.

The principle "always act through the motive of love" is absolute and cannot be added to intellectually except in redundant ways. What love is must be comprehended by the will as well as by the intellect; hence there must be a way to address the will which is included in the mind but is more than the mere intellect. The basic language of the will is that of experience rather than of formulas; just as in a stable faith, which is a dynamic combination of will and intellect, love is evoked by the fact of love in history and an admonition to consistency about it. In "speaking the language" of the will, actual love is empirically evoked first; this provides the will with a field for consistency other than that of mere discourse.

Love must develop in terms of an 'honesty' (integrity) which includes discursive objectivity but surpasses it. Discursive objectivity has only the duty to acknowledge the reality or truth of obvious facts and propositions; it needs only to describe well. Honesty or sincerity of the will includes objectivity but goes beyond it (chapter 4). Often where the intellect cannot detect the presence of wilfulness, will can detect is own wilfulness through the medium of sincere belief, i.e. the active relationship of intellect and will. For example, love is often counterfeited by sentimentality because it has not been checked by its own moral implications (I Cor. 13:4—8). As a means of detecting these moral counterfeits, there is often in the morally sensitive person what is called "the still small voice" or "an arresting tick" (11:220), which detects subtle self-deception overlooked by the object-centered intellect.

Once the will can capture the "arresting tick" of self-criticism, it may be able to discern the link between the very faint image and a stronger but more obscure element of will from which the faint element derived its being. It is in this sense of holding the "arresting tick" or "still small voice" that the will plays a stabilizing role, through sincere belief, in making the vague and hidden motivational presuppositions of our moral being subsumable under principles; only at this point can ordinary objectivity come into play. Frequently the will in the form of sincere belief is alone able to detect other beliefs which are morally counterfeit, e.g. believing sentimentality is love. Furthermore, it is in this area that certain moral principles, in spite of their logical unity, are found to be inadequate for men of action who live in a one-chance moral world, instead of in the retreats of ethical scholasticism.

The areas of moral objectivity that are beyond demonstration, whether experiential or logical, must be treated as a matter of sincerity or honesty. Often these pre-demonstrable moral issues are crucial but so unrationalistic that only the will, through sincere belief, can capture their essence long enough to see where the issue of sincere responsibility begins, in order to trace these ethereal but powerful motives to their more objective relations and connections.

In summary, belief stabilizes in the sense that it takes pre-knowledge factors or experiences and holds them in a manner that permits criticism to test them for their positive or negative value. If belief did not objectify pre-moral values, giving them a fair chance to enter the moral realm, there would be no moral advance in humanity; all advance in values must begin as belief stabilizes and holds them for critical attention.

The language of the sincere will has a strong tendency toward the experiential level (even if the experience is pre-rational, i.e. not yet analyzable into the categories of ordinary experience). It is like a true faith that, seeking to proceed from experience wherever possible, avoids speculation but still sees where belief must enter if there is to be any moral advance or creativity.

The ideological, or 'the prophetic,' element of Christianity has demonstrated the greatest sensitivity and proficiency in speaking the language that penetrates and activates the will on moral principles. It recognizes that principles, although not as negative as laws, play a quasi-negative role. It is at this point that many ethical thinkers have failed to see that the negative is only one side of the moral life; much moral philosophy, for the same reason, has consigned itself to a purely static role and consequently is inadequate for an age of ideology and atomic energy.

CHAPTER 6

THE DYNAMIC FACTORS OF A
MORAL IDEOLOGY

Basic Characteristics of Dynamic Morality

The Existence of Dynamic Morality.—This chapter proceeds on two basic ethical assumptions. First, it is presupposed that a dynamic morality does exist (Ap. 97) ; that it is a proper subject for moral philosophy (Ap. 98) ; and consequently that if moral theories cannot deal with these empirical, dynamic elements, it is not because of the unreality of dynamic morality but is due to the inadequacy of our method of theorizing. Second, it is assumed that dynamic morality is to be preferred to static morality, if it both includes and surpasses the best stabilizing elements of the static system (7:37, 38).

A dynamic form of morality is centered in the belief, well attested to in human history, that there is a dynamic level of moral living based upon moral wholeness, and that all of the dynamic elements in the human psyche should be channeled into the same direction toward the most worthy goals. This presupposes a relational approach to the moral life (Preface and Ap. 1) where the world-view is a proper synthesis of knowing and believing, where the *dynamic* is a proper synthesis of value-beliefs and doing, where the methodology is a proper synthesis of doing and knowing, and where world-view, *dynamic,* and methodology work together in a dynamic unity toward a creative moral advance of mankind.

The moral life requires an element of dynamic prior to norms in somewhat the same sense that, according to many philosophers, value theory is prior to ethics. A dynamic moral philosophy is based on the premise that an actual *dynamic* (which centers in felt-values but is not limited to them) is operative prior to the framework (psychological and theoretical) which is needed to harness and channel the dynamic; it is like Watt's discovery of the *dynamic* of steam before he made the theoretical and mechanical framework to bring order out of it. This priority is temporal; logically the norms must precede moral action. Both forms of priority must be taken as major considerations.

The acceptance of the temporal priority of moral *dynamic* forbids that moral philosophy, beyond certain methodological considerations, be prejudiced towards naturalism. *Dynamic* involves felt-values; but there is a level of ideological conviction that goes beyond 'felt-value' as this term is commonly used in current writings (Ap. 99). Certain ideological goals of the most extensive humanitarian character are able to raise the intensity of feeling quality in felt-values to a level that approaches or equals conviction; this conviction is able to gain great strength without being dogmatic because of the impetus and balance arising from the relational rigor of a moral ideology. This relational rigor consists of a balanced relation of knowing, believing, and doing through a proper prior relation of will and intellect. A moral ideology makes a unique contribution to the testing of the dynamic level of felt-values, both because of its rigor in testing value norms for sufficient frictionlessness, and because of its breadth of actual encounter with immoral and irrational ideologies, which gives it an empirical measurement of the adequacy of philosophical moral sanctions in major world issues.

It is ideologically inadequate to hold that a scale of felt-values is the only source of basic decision, because some decisions cannot wait for felt-value; we worship the Creator rather than the creature (Rom. 1:18—25), for instance, in consequence of a decision that is prior to a valid scale of spiritual values. A moral ideology must thereby relate this exception to the usual rule for constructing scales of value, since immoral ideologies make it a point to find the moral loopholes in the dogmatically naturalistic approaches.

The Dynamic of Freedom from Self-Concerned Calculation.— A dynamic morality is dynamic by its lack of need of self-concerned calculation; it finds its own development through commitment to the dynamic moral development of others. It is commitment-centered, i.e. decision before the fact, or committing oneself to the right before its demands are particularized. It is centered in the positive attitude of 'what will help,' the basis of volitional sincerity.

Dynamic morality faces the inertia of the human will (Ap. 100) ; moral principles that do not take this into account are inadequate. It recognizes, on the one hand, that the will exists as a *dynamic* and must be channeled by the intellect and not the intellect channeled by the will; it also recognizes, on the other hand, that the intellect's "dynamic" is not adequate by itself. The "dynamic" of the intellect in logic or fact is more like unmovableness; morality implies a moving or change of fact on the basis of purposeful decision according to the demands of moral norms.

There is a dynamic level of morality that possesses high efficiency because it is free from the need to wander about in the often broad leeway that even the best moral principles must allow. This is what we might call "the spirit of discernment," i.e. the perception of what is most suitably creative out of several normatively acceptable choices.

The Dynamic of Basic Moral Decision.—The decision to be on a dynamic level is a basic essential of dynamic morality. One actual case of dynamic morality is all it takes to establish it as a fact; for example, once someone accomplishes a great, dynamic moral fete as an established fact, it becomes a challenge to decision as much as any other fact of the moral life. To ignore it purposely would in reality be a decision of rejection; therefore the only alternative would be to channel any newly created moral *dynamic* by the highest possible norms. It is like the case where once someone had demonstrated his ability to swim the English Channel; this forever became an established fact of challenge to all adventurous swimmers. Likewise once a Socrates or a St. Francis lives a new level of moral *dynamic* before his fellow men, the latter have no choice but either to betray the light this dynamic morality brings or channel it according to acceptable moral norms; either choice is a decision, but the latter may be creatively *dynamic*.

A dynamic morality is centered in decision that creates something new at the same time it stabilizes the practical role of norms. The decision to accept moral absolutes is not the same as being limited by them, just as a musician plays by the notes, but is not limited by the illusion that the notes are everything to the art of making music.

Dynamic decision is not made purely by decision, but involves belief or faith (Ap. 101). There is only one proper decision about facts as such and that is to accept them as facts and to treat them so; nevertheless there is much that remains where the facts cannot go (for example, the future and issues that can never attain more than cognitive probability) which must be classed as belief but still demands dynamic moral decision. What is sure is already fact, and hence has little need of *dynamic* to establish its actuality. Dynamic moral issues, however, involve a normatively acceptable changing or modifying of factual conditions toward higher goals through justified belief.

If a dynamic morality is to be truly moral, it must be rightly related to objectivity. However, objectivity about decision (i.e. consistency in the will of the subject) is not the same as scientific objectivity; objectivity about decision involves the fact that one cannot be detached, whereas scientific objectivity demands detachment because it is about fact, and hence descriptive. The objectivity of moral decision deals with what ought to be; hence, it cannot be detached from commitment to norms nor from the creation of the factual goals implied by the value system or ideology that stays within the moral bounds of these norms; otherwise it would be dead.

Dynamic morality makes decisions that draw, whereas static morality demands (7:34). Any morality that includes an adequate sanction is dynamic to the extent that it is empirically adequate, that is, when all can testify to the personal adequacy of the norm. A norm is not a moral norm until it enters the decision procedure of men; theories about norms do not become human norms only by the thinking or talking about them; they must be engaged in a moral decision procedure (Ap. 102). A dynamic morality is found in specific men (7:34) ; to date, all intellectualizations of this have been generalizations which arose as a result of how these men had lived dynamic morality as a fact. These morally dynamic men learned to channel existing dynamic forces through consistency, for example, principles; consistency or singlemindedness is the heart of dynamic morality.

118

Moral Ideology as the Experimental Link
Relating Theoretical Moral Norms
to Moral Action

A moral ideology is dynamic by definition (chapter 4) ; actually it is dynamic by its capacity to sustain certain vital relations necessary to the moral life that are not sustained by merely intellectualistic systems. If moral philosophers prefer static systems, there is nothing more to say; but if they realize that only conceptual moral schemes which are not inherently hostile to the dynamic side of the moral life are capable of meeting the problems of this age, then they must recognize that an adequate experimental laboratory is needed to test the capacity of theoretical norms to include or relate to moral *dynamic,* and hence to moral action. A moral ideology serves as a bridge between moral theory and moral action in a fashion that gives theory more *dynamic* and the action more normative rigor; this kind of ideology is therefore the most efficient laboratory to test the necessary relatedness of moral theories to moral action in at least six major areas, (1) survival of norms, (2) relational concreteness, (3) volitional sincerity, (4) extensive, coherent responsibility, (5) unavoidability of decision, and (6) creative moral advance.

Survival of Norms.—An ethical norm is obligated to survive on the basis of its human adequacy to give a rational channel to moral *dynamic* and to be non-interfering with elements of moral creativity, even to the point of being superseded by a better norm.

Mankind has reached the era in human history where the survival of ethical norms is being threatened by evil ideologies through extensive techniques of mass brainwashing. Norms that are adequate for this age must possess the resources or relationships that insure their own survival. For example, they should hold a functional relationship to a moral ideology which is superior, in its power and effectiveness in preserving moral norms, to the ideologies that are out to destroy the role of moral norms in the affairs of men and nations.

Relational Concreteness.—Just as a moral ideology is centered in its relatedness to concrete moral action, a dynamic moral philosophy must likewise possess the conceptual framework of such a

119

relatedness. The moral ideology is therefore the best laboratory to test this relational concreteness of the normative system as to whether it can sustain moral advancement in particular cases on a worldwide scale, i.e. any particular case where there is willingness.

This relational concreteness in a dynamic morality is incompatible with certain philosophical attitudes; for example, it cannot be an isolated discipline and still preserve its sources of dynamic; nor can it either presuppose the limits of its own extensiveness, except in rejecting contradictions, or be dominated by an opportunistic, intellectualistic metaphysics of reductionistic convenience.

A moral ideology is furthermore the most efficient laboratory to test a moral theory on the grounds of relational concreteness, in that many moral theories presuppose implicitly an individualistic egoism that is not revealed until they are put into an ideological context. In the ideological context the will usually cannot hide behind impressive but harmful mental system-building that abstracts and complicates moral truth to the point where decision becomes hampered in spite of the logical unity of the system.

Unnecessary complications of systems are often excused with the contention that they are not intended for the average consumer in his practical moral life; it is suggested, moreover, that such systems are a reservoir of coherent thought from which the professional moralist may deduce his rules and maxims. Such arguments, however, are often a form of moral sacerdotalism that complicates ethical norms unduly by making it necessary to have mediators between rational thought about moral norms and sincere moral action. Relational concreteness occurs when the moral agent himself can go clearly and intelligently from universal norms to particular moral action. The need of professional mediators is more likely the fault of the ethical theory rather than the average moral agent (Ap. 103).

Simplicity is an essential element in a concrete (i.e. un-abstract), dynamic morality, even though this morality is formal. For example, the morality of the Pharisees in the time of Jesus was most complicated and very static; it was a morality of energy-sapping rationalization, just as many systems are today. These rationalists spent much of their mental resources trying to decide such questions as "who is my neighbor?" before they could get to the business of doing good. Jesus wiped out the need of their rationalism by the simplicity-begetting standard of the sanctity of all persons, given implicitly in the admonition to love even one's enemies and to be a neighbor wherever the need presents itself. Moral universalism has a simplicity because of its inclusion, not in spite of it. Total commitment of the will is of the same nature. However, those who neglect *dynamic* usually miss this kind of volitional totality.

An essential part of this dynamic simplicity is the objective of its appeal. Too often the philosophers have missed this in their appeal to an intellectual elite whose supposed existence draws the moral battle-line in the wrong place, and very indistinctly in many crucial areas. A dynamic appeal must not be a source of confusion to those who have the good will to obey; it is primarily aimed at the obeyers.

Any extensive study in the area of the relation of moral norms to practical moral obedience will disclose the importance of concrete will in the form of justified belief, i.e. beliefs criticized to the point that they come in dynamic sequence. Dynamic sequence implies that a philosophical moral system first must be able to deal with the necessary volitional presuppositions of its universal norms; for example, if the norm is universal love, the sequence is to make love operative in at least one person first on the basis of universal norms, lest the whole issue of concreteness become a farce. The universal must be deducible to a specific case of actuality; I am suspicious that certain egoistic ethical norms like hedonism are much more recalcitrant on the level of specific application than most of its theoretic proponents surmise, because of the wrong normative (volitional) order inherent in egoism as such.

It takes a moral ideology to put some of the higher implications of moral norms into an efficient, dynamic order that makes the best form of volitional organization. Psychology is a great asset here, but it is not adequate alone because of the limitations of its naturalistic methodology. A moral ideology therefore serves as an organizer for efficient execution of the extra-naturalistic modes of the higher moral norms; it also serves as the best empirical test of the pragmatic proficiency of norms by relating them to particular moral action in a universal variety of particular circumstances.

Volitional Sincerity.—A basic element of volitional sincerity is the commitment to norms that are capable of totalistic application to the most universal perversions of the human will. On a humanitarian level this would be the capacity to deal with all forms of human betrayal to norms, such as the sanctity of the person. On a religious (for example, Christian) level it would be the capacity to deal with the betrayal of *agape;* I say "betrayal" because sincerity or the lack of it presupposes some prior commitment to the norms in question. Intellectualistic objectivity may be a matter of a methodology; but volitional sincerity is a matter of the good life itself which cannot be manipulated or rejected on convenience, or even for methodological reasons.

Volitional insincerity may conceivably arise in altruism; however, it is more likely to arise in a climate of ethical egoism. It is difficult for the will to be sincere when it is guided by norms that have, in spite of their intellectual rigor, inherent will-complicating elements. For example, both ideological Christianity and Marxism-Leninism have come to the same conclusion, in spite of their different moral views, concerning the unnecessary volitional complications that egoism begets. Egoism tends to be ultimately self-contradictory like dishonesty, and any developed ideology is inclined to discover this incoherence *de facto* as it bridges the gap between theory and action.

Much volitional insincerity arises from the misconception that complete and fervid opinionatedness on a point constitutes sincerity, for example, that the inquisitors showed their sincerity through their persistence and zeal in spite of their being wrong; this kind of thinking misses the point of volitional sincerity by lacking consideration of the basic need of other human wills. Some of the most zealous efforts of men have turned into colossal crimes against human personality because men have wilfully identified their beliefs with infallible knowledge; volitional sincerity forbids this through a relationally clear idea of the person which includes the relation of will with other wills and will with intellect.

The idea of the person is a norm and a formal element, but not an abstraction. If it includes only intellect, it is necessarily abstract, but if it has realistic inclusion of will, then it does not need to be abstract. Will cannot be abstracted without distorting it;

hence will must be seen in its believing role (i.e. belief being the living combination of intellect and will) if it is a rational will above the animal level. A valid idea of the person must include a related, concrete will in its living form, i.e. justified belief which does not usurp the role of knowledge.

Belief does not have to be sincere to be merely a dynamic force in ideologies such as scientism or Marxism. But it must be sincere in order to be dynamic and *moral*. Only a moral ideology tests certain levels of belief extensively and concretely enough to determine its sincerity, and only an ideology which presupposes universal sincerity as a norm is moral. It takes the volitional equivalent of an ideology to relate beliefs to one another on a scale that can properly test their most extensive volitional aspects; social philosophies and religions seek to do this, but often on a level that stifles commitment for the sake of mores and ritual.

If there are such things as *a priori* or universal values (I believe there are), then the belief-centered Christian ideology has done more to discover them than intellectualistic theory because, as an ideology of faith, it has been successful in actually uniting the wills that grasp the theoretical values. Uniting will successfully on a broad scale is more difficult than uniting intellects, and its success indicates the discovery of common values of sincerity (for example, unselfishness, Ap. 104). Essentially, value is will channeled and criticized by intellect. Uniting wills successfully on a level that goes beyond point-of-view indicates the discovery of the "methodology" of the will; this discovery is based upon the sincere attitude of giving good will absolute priority over "what I want," or "want to think."

Sincere good will begins on a firm foundation only when men know their own natures well. Sincerity about one's own moral needs begets a simplicity that is most dynamic in its effects in benefiting others, in comparison to the petrification that generally results from moral rationalism. One may know the nature of persons only through the path of knowing the nearest person, himself.

Hence, it is unwise to neglect the role of volitional sincerity in the moral life, which is gained through the kind of relational fullness that only justified belief can give. It is the necessary link between universal norms within the mind of the moral agent and concrete action by the moral agent worthy of universal emulation. Although volitional sincerity is by no means limited to a moral ideology, it is best tested and nurtured by a moral ideology or its volitional equivalent.

Extensive Coherent Responsibility.—A moral ideology is the most efficient laboratory to test an ethical theory on the grounds of its capacity for the conceptual inclusion of extensive, coherent responsibility. It tests the ethical theory as to whether it fosters or retards the volitional sense of responsibility (56:94, 95, 145, 148, 149, 153) (for example, a morality centered in equal rights is negative). No ethical systems openly advocate a lack of responsibility, but a number of them, if put within the laboratory of a moral ideology, would fail to exhibit a mature degree of volitional responsibility. Instances of this are ethical emotivism and social approbative systems.

'Freedom' is often an intellectualized reduction from the fact of responsibility; actually, as the Marxist-Leninists have so ably demonstrated, the conviction of responsibility does not need an overdrawn intellectualization of freedom. To start from an intellectualization of freedom is to begin with a norm that can be full of rationalistic friction to the highest level of moral creativity. Furthermore, it is a norm which, if made to play the positive role in morality, is easily open to ideological manipulation by immoral ideologies (84:182, 268, 299).

Freedom is absolutely necessary as a quasi-negative concept, but the fact of freedom arises from a more basic element of responsibility. Responsibility creates actual freedom in an effortless way through its ideological competence to avoid being used as an ideological tool by ideologies and motives that are of an inferior moral level.

Responsibility encompasses the need of clarity in the volitional and ideological implications of an idea over and above the ability of that idea to withstand the formal test; on this basis, it is able to establish much greater social coherence without the energy and time consuming rationalism that doctrinal 'freedom' requires. When the concept 'freedom' is used as a moral causal factor, it frequently produces more isolated individualism than social coherence. True freedom is established through functioning responsibility extending itself to a universal level to include all men, not by a spread of the speculative concept of freedom.

On the individual level freedom is found only in an ideology or philosophy of life which is responsible enough to make total demands on the will so that singlemindedness becomes a concrete reality in individual men.

> The will responds to total demands. It has peace only when there is singleness of purpose demanding total effort. Its basic need is to give everything for something great. (14:16)

It took a moral ideology to discover this fact, a fact that is vaguely presupposed by most ethical theories but made clearly explicit by its empirical testing within the extensive moral laboratory that only an ideology (or its equivalent) can give.

The fact of responsibility entails freedom by its inherent obligation to instill or inspire responsibility in all men. Men only develop volitional responsibility by being free to make their own decisions; therefore responsibility is the more stable and creative concept. The speculative concept of freedom is sub-moral in many cases because it is not an implication of conscience but an abstract negation of mechanistic determinism. Moral theories which implicitly suggest this type of abstract freedom (for example, certain highly intellectualistic theories) are very quickly detected as volitionally inadequate when given an empirical workout by a moral ideology. The ideology generally reveals that moral systems based on abstract freedom have either no *dynamic* or too much of it toward the wrong things.

Responsibility is dynamic in the sense that it is an ideological concept which ethical theories must presuppose within the will of those who accept these theories; its *dynamic* depends upon the sincerity of its goal and the concreteness of application. Some ethical theories make responsibility reductionistic and thus eliminate its ideological creative power. The result is that these reductionistic systems cannot imply guilt (Ap. 105) on a level that can move the human will on particular issues. Any dynamic morality is polar (Ap. 106) in this respect. What assures the will of moral rightness

125

on an extensive degree must correspondingly produce an equal *dynamic* of moral convincement of guilt where this positive conviction is betrayed, especially on the particular level.

Hence the test of an ethical theory, on the grounds of responsibility, is how it fosters a clear concept that is logically coherent, and also the extensiveness of the theory within particular persons so as to cover the complete breadth and depth of their experience in order that they may know the relation of their moral norms to every one of their experiences. A moral ideology is the most efficient stimulation to this extensiveness of responsibility into all areas of life; it is also the best test of whether our theoretical ethical ideas and norms are realistic in concrete cases.

The Unavoidability of Decision.—A moral ideology is the most efficient laboratory to test an ethical theory because it recognizes and is constructed on the premise that decision is unavoidable (Ap. 107). Ideology is a fact and much of it that confronts contemporary men and nations forces moral decision by its very presence. The decision of response to immoral ideologies is either ideologically adequate or something ideologically inferior, regardless of the label we put on our philosophy of social response. Any moral system is inadequate that does not take into account the fact that decision is unavoidable, for example, scientistic systems. These systems might be more sympathetic to well-reasoned belief if they gave proper recognition to the unavoidability of decision.

There is much faulty and fragmentary thinking concerning the nature of human decision. Much of the fault is due to efforts to deal with the nature of decision in terms of a purely logical and descriptive methodology. These factors are unquestionably necessary, but they deal more with the situations that precede and follow the decision rather than the decision itself. One does not penetrate very deeply into the nature of decision when he conceives of decision merely in terms of atomic acts, as he might so conceive a terminating judgment about some particular direct experience (51: 203) ; decision has to be seen from the vantage point of a commitment in order to penetrate its basic nature. On the isolated level it is almost impossible to distinguish decision from mere desire. Isolated decisions are very real, but they must be related to each other by some general decision or commitment if any meaning is to be given to the moral life; on any lesser basis they are merely data for psychology.

Until decision is put on a shared level in a community of decision (ideology), it can easily be counterfeited by desire, particularly if the ethical norms that guide it are scientistic, relativistic, or reductionistic. Ideology distinguishes the emotive (desire) from the volitional or from commitment (decision) by its extensiveness of application. Happiness and egoistic theories cannot hold decision on an extensive scale, since one does not need to decide to be happy or egoistic for himself; most of the genuinely happy people that I know have gained it as a result of aiming at something much greater. These theories cannot beget consistent moral growth because they depend more upon outer circumstance than upon inner decisional principle. Just as a community of scholars reveals subjectivism in the intellect, a community of wills (ideology) reveals whether "decisions" are objective commitments or mere subjective desires. Objective concepts about the right are not yet objective decisions about the right. Logic judges the former, whereas it takes an ideological framework to give the most extensive test to the latter.

Even if an ethical norm does justice to the logical nature of the intellect, this does not necessarily imply that the same norm can do full justice to the nature of the human will in its decision procedure. Full justice to the decision procedure is an empirical matter which demands the comparative testing possible only within a relational or ideological framework. One's genuineness or sincerity in the moral realm is measured essentially by his actual (empirical) willingness to "get up" immediately if he does "fall down" concerning his standards. A baby's desire to walk is not measured by his falls but by how quickly and eagerly he tries to get up; the same is the case concerning our knowledge of whether our commitment to moral norms is real decision or merely desire.

The role of knowledge in the decision procedure of the moral life lies essentially in one's cognitive assurance of both the reality of moral norms and the reality of his own decision to apply these norms to his own value and ideological goals. He must know the binding nature of his own commitment to the highest standards of moral objectivity of mind and sincerity of will.

127

The moral agent must also know, as far as possible, that he is not betraying the role of belief in the moral life and that he is subscribing to the most credible form of ontological and pragmatic belief available; the necessity of decision and its corresponding responsibility implies the necessity of intelligent belief (Ap. 108). Belief is the only form of cognition open to man concerning the yet unseen results of his present decisions. The morally intelligent person knows how to make his moral knowledge of the past cooperate on an epistemologically sound basis with his belief-centered decision procedure. Those who try to avoid the role of belief usually end up by unwittingly serving some of the lower forms of belief like scientism and emotivism.

In order to be the highest type, justified belief must function on an equal plane with the belief complexes of a moral ideology. A moral ideology is channeled by moral norms of the highest order; a moral ideology also works in reciprocal fashion by judging these moral norms on a pragmatic level, i.e. judging how these norms contribute to cooperation with the dynamic forces of morally sound human goals. Some moral norms provide much less "friction" than others do to the moral decision procedure by eliminating the confusion that results from such dynamic-sapping principles as egoism, relativism, and scientism, which are often hidden as implicit premises in otherwise logically sound moral norms. On the ideological level, moral norms representing *eros* (i.e. enlightened egoism) have a radical lack of dynamic force in comparison with *agape;* even the Marxist-Leninists, in their recent literature (Ap. 109), unwittingly reveal some insight on this fact. It cannot be known, however, by those who employ the methods of ethical scholasticism. The test of the adequacy of moral decision is primarily by reference to moral norms; but since decision is unavoidable, it must also be tested on the level of volitional adequacy. Decision meets its final and most difficult test in the field of mobilized will, that is, in the field of ideology, or its morally dynamic equivalent. If ethical norms imply decisions, then these norms themselves should be tested for their human applicability and adequacy on this level, because the moral life has no second chance.

Creative Moral Advance.—Finally, a moral ideology is the most efficient laboratory to test the efficiency of an ethical theory on the criterion of harmony with the creative moral advance that comes only through well-reasoned belief. Beliefs have traditionally held a secondary role in Western philosophy except where they could be euphemized or disguised as knowledge. Kant euphemized moral beliefs by calling them by the same name as something rigorous and cognitively respectable, i.e. practical reason. The positivists have reversed this process by identifying moral belief semantically with something that is undependable and vague, i.e. emotion. The proper procedure is to let moral belief stand on its own merit, without euphemism or pejoration, and be allowed to exhibit itself as to its true role in shaping the corrigible future for the significant needs of human life.

Belief has never had what I term the 'pistological' treatment (*pistis:* Gk., belief) it needs by philosophers in general (Ap. 110). Philosophers have usually avoided the positive role of belief and have thereby missed its importance within the creative side of moral philosophy. Those who have accepted belief as central have too often used it as an excuse to neglect the necessary role of rigorous moral and epistemological norms. Getting belief and normative rigor together takes clear moral perception that has been well-seasoned in the real world of moral encounter considerably beyond the realms of ethical scholasticism.

In this century it has become almost an accepted truism that the so-called "knowledge" men have to live by is belief which is well-reasoned or justified. In perception, it is now extensively recognized that it is the cognitive and inferential component that is corrigible (52:26, 27). This element of flexibility is the root of its creativity. Rational moral norms must test the justifiability of creative beliefs, but moral norms themselves are essentially quasi-negative and serve to channel creative beliefs. Norms may even play the role of unjustified belief when they are forced into the dynamic role that only certain value or ideological beliefs can play.

Once creative beliefs associated with moral action become factually established in society, they may imply new norms more adequate than those which formerly channeled these beliefs. The newer norms do not violate the old ones; they supersede them in efficiency by being more 'frictionless' to the will, as tested in an ideological context. This 'frictionlessness' may appear as a sanction but it is really a quasi-negative factor giving the implicit value and belief *dynamics* an easier path. Certain moral norms are friction-causing because they have not taken the full nature of the will into account. If the norms in question were adequately tested and proved on a volitional basis, they would be capable of central and obvious deductions of decision-fostering elements on a non-egoistic level, for example, humility. Adequate ideological testing reveals that humility is not as central in the deductions from the norm of pure duty as it is from *agape*. Likewise, sensivity to deepest human needs cannot be central in deductions from norms that give egoism a logical refuge.

The moral life cannot operate without belief if it is to include the process of inference (52:28), but even after a moral system provides a place for justified belief, it must also have pragmatic criteria through which such justified beliefs may be ranked according to their capacity to produce responsible moral action. Bergson has done much to show that there is a dynamic side to the moral life, which many ethical thinkers miss (7:34, 35, 38, 39, 40, 47, 55, 59, 60, 61, 63, 65, 77, 78, 97), that is produced by a creative unity or singlemindedness which cannot be limited merely to the need for logical unity on the basis of norms.

It is difficult to discover this *dynamic* unless we accept certain basic beliefs. The first of these is, that the moral life must be a volitional unity as well as an intellectual unity. This volitional unity itself is a unity of our whole system of beliefs and motives, i.e. "purity of heart." Thus the presence of false or unjustified beliefs will threaten man's moral unity and the quality of *dynamic* it brings. Gabriel Marcel pointedly refers to the prevalence at present of a lack of inner unity:

> Modern man, ever since the Renaissance, seems to have lived in a kind of anarchy. The different parts of his existence, his personal, political, family, religious and social life resemble semi-independent kingdoms ruled by different laws which, even if they do not completely contradict each other, yet have nothing in common. So twentieth-century man manages to be a rationalist in philosophy, practising in religion, a 'realist' in business, a democrat in politics and a dictator in the home.

All the success of modern ideologies can be explained by

130

the inner desire of modern man to reach wholeness. But all that is most profound in man rebels against these efforts, because in all attempts so far some essential aspect of his nature has been left out . . .

Many put their faith in the success of conferences or intellectual exchanges. Others placed their hopes in the ascendancy of certain men whose very memory is now despised. Others clung to an empty idealism which was soon smashed like foam on the rock-life facts of everyday life. Everything has been tried in an effort to avoid a change in man himself. (63:162, 164)

It is difficult to possess moral unity and wholeness (54:93, 94) unless one's beliefs about the moral life, as it actually is, are realistic. The dynamic side of morality cannot begin without facing the existing hinderances to the moral life itself, for example man's unwillingness to change, which is a major form of human perversity. C. I. Lewis says,

If this overarching principle anywhere fails of acknowledgment, that should merely remind us that human perversity is as perennial as the rationality it belies. The consequences of that fact would be even more serious than they are, if it were not that rationality makes for unanimity whereas perversities are various and likely to cancel one another. And if moral perversity is more frequent than perverse repudiation of other rational insights, and history more frequently shows recurrence of moral barbarism than of other forms of stupidity and obliquity, that too has its explanation. Moral enlightenment meets a resistance which other forms of learning do not: we inherit savage propensities of behaviour which call for our restraint, as likewise we inherit inclination to the imprudent; but we are born innocent of beliefs. Criticism is always harder to take than information, even when it is self-criticism. (54:93, 94)

The first step of a dynamic morality is to begin where men are. This involves a belief-attitude that does not need a rationalistic measure of our perversity or the lack of it in order to apply a moral solution. Moreover, it is a belief-attitude of decision to give the whole intellect and will to the most creative moral change possible within oneself regardless of his past attainments or the comparative lack of moral attainment in his fellows. Creative morality implies change in human nature and, of necessity, in particular men (7:99).

Change in human nature is a concept that is becoming more widely accepted among some of the world's statesmen (Adenauer, Kishi, U Nu, and others), as the only reasonable solution of some of the gigantic moral problems man has created for himself. In order to do justice in our acceptance or rejection of this idea that 'human nature can change,' men must be clear about its implications on the three basic levels of concept, belief, and commitment.

On the conceptual level, a clear idea of what human nature is must be understood in terms of its basic virtues and vices. Respecting its virtues, one can no longer afford to assume the shallow rationalism of the Enlightenment, nor can he presuppose the argumentative morbidities of Calvinism concerning its vices. There are no rational grounds why human nature cannot find a general marked improvement worthy of the word 'change'.

On the belief level, the possibility of change in human nature has been the basic presupposition of the moralities that have demonstrated their dynamic capabilities on a broad empirical scale. Of late, philosophical ethical theories have usually neglected a critical examination of this question by simply resting their views on what man's thoughts of moral norms ought to be, leaving what man's nature actually is to the descriptive sciences of psychology and sociology. However, a well-reasoned belief that human nature ought to change cannot be derived from the collected data of the descriptive sciences on human behavior. Such a belief is normative and ideal; and although it involves the best knowledge available, it must be vitalized by a basic and irreducible belief in the creative centrality of the category of the holy (Ap. 111).

A belief in the possibility of a change in man, not merely in his environment, is inevitably associated with a dynamic moral force that attracts rather than compels. Bergson says,

> Why is it, then, that saints have their imitators, and why do the great moral leaders draw the masses after them? They ask nothing, and yet they receive. They have no need to exhort; their mere existence suffices. For such is precisely the nature of this other morality. Whereas natural obligation is a pressure or a propulsive force, complete and perfect morality has the effect of an appeal. (7:34)

132

The Dynamic Factors of a Moral Ideology

A dynamic moral ideology abounds in the kind of justified belief that vitalizes the decision procedure. A classic example of this is the belief in the sanctity of the person (Ap. 112). This belief involves the acceptance of an obligation to change every element of human nature that betrays this norm, which elements are legion. This task begins with individual commitment and ends with mobilized, united will on a global scale according to moral norms, i.e. in a moral ideology or its philosophically dynamic equivalent. The norms channel the ideology and the ideology demonstrates the relevance of the norms to this age and the kind of human nature we actually have. Too many moral theories are designed for an abstract idealization of human nature; they have no real application because they seek to take man from where he is not. A man's capability to deal with ideological issues is an excellent index of his moral objectivity and sincerity about where he actually is in his own nature.

On the commitment level, change in human nature involves basic volitional sincerity, the will to change it unreservedly and the determination to begin the process of changing it with oneself. This is the heart of any dynamic moral ideology, a *dynamic* that makes the transformation of human nature the most creative of all the arts.

CONCLUSION

Because of the unavoidability of moral decision, the most important function of contemporary moral philosophy is to be normatively and dynamically adequate in its encounter with the deepest moral needs of men and nations. Since the most crucial world problems are essentially ideological, this will require a moral philosophy capable of displacing the attempts of immoral ideologies on a universal scale. Actively speaking this is a moral ideology (or its equivalent by any other name) ; conceptually speaking this is a dynamic moral philosophy that includes a relational approach corresponding to that of a moral ideology. Ideology and moral philosophy still have their distinctive roles to play: the former centers in the mobilization of will (justified belief in action), and the latter centers in the systematization of concepts; but there is no distinct division between a moral ideology and a dynamic moral philosophy. The moral ideology is a relational bridge between moral norms and moral action; thereby it serves as the most efficient laboratory to test the dynamic adequacy of moral norms and the normative rigor of moral action.

APPENDIX 1

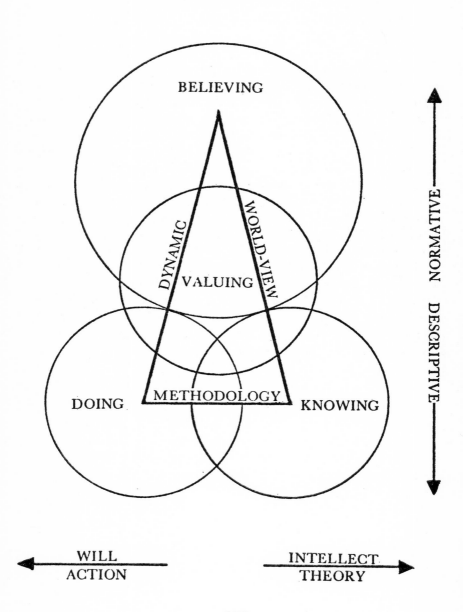

APPENDICES

1. My usage of the concept 'relational' centers in my notion that analysis, even though it is an essential element to moral philosophy, is not adequate by itself; moral philosophy needs an equal amount of synthesis through a balanced relating of its various cognitive and volitional components, in a fashion that begets the *dynamic* necessary to meet current moral issues on a universal scale. The preceding diagram shows how the essential elements of a moral ideology (the sides of the triangle) relate the essential areas of the cognitive-volitional process (the circles). It takes an ideology, or its equivalent, both to effect a balanced relation of these cognitive-volitional areas, and to test the pragmatic effectiveness produced by a proper balance of this relation in the world of actual moral encounter. The area of common inclusion in the circles of knowing, valuing, and doing is the cognitive heart of a moral ideology; it designates the area of universally valid moral norms (for example, the golden rule) which we know, we value (a form of belief), and we do if we are men of sound mind and good will; the sole task of a moral ideology is to marshal all legitimate forms of knowing, believing, and doing to activate these moral *a prioris* universally.

2. An epistemological definition of 'ideology': an ideology constitutes the vital relationship of knowing, believing (including valuing), and doing in a manner that gives normative cognition a broad range of application and a solid empirical foundation of testability, in contrast to the less relational and more narrow approach of Western intellectualism.

3. A methodological definition of 'ideology': an ideology is the systematic use of ideas as tools and weapons; it is the mobilization of will on a social scale towards an ideal goal.

4. An ontological definition of 'ideology': an ideology is the living and dynamic link between knowing, believing, and doing.

5. An ideological definition of 'ideology': an ideology is a

137

life's purpose in action on a world scale in order to change the world to a new level of existence.

6. A wholistic definition of 'ideology': an ideology is constituted by a world-view, a *dynamic,* and a methodology in a vitally balanced relationship founded upon the moral and social needs of the age.

7. Believing includes most but not all of the area of valuing, since certain basic value concepts may rightly be classed as knowledge.

8. Paton gives us his view of the contemporary philosophical scene in general:

> But philosophical thinking about science is to be sharply distinguished from science itself, since it is concerned with the nature and validity of the principles on which scientific thinking proceeds. If this difference is admitted, there is no reason why philosophy should not similarly concern itself with the principles of art and morality and politics and history and religion. Even if it were confined to the study of language, the use of which is only one of the human activities in which rational principles are manifested, it would still be arbitrary to concentrate on the language of science and ignore all the others.
>
> This more catholic view is, it seems to me, gradually winning acceptance. Unless it does so, I should fear even in this sober country a lapse into existentialism, which is one way of reacting against an over-emphasis on science and against a narrow intellectualism which confuses reasoning with rationality. It is always easy to predict events after they have happened, but one lesson to be drawn from the history of the last fifty years is that no one is likely to foretell in what direction philosophy will move next. My hope is that the wider sympathies of recent years will lead to more comprehensive and more synoptic philosophies; for although we are all agreed that one task of philosophy is to clear up particular muddles, I cannot believe that this is enough. (55:353)

It is no less scientific to say that these moral matters should also be examined within their living contexts than to say that a zoologist should also study his specimens in their living habitat as well as on the anatomy table.

9. Hofstadter on the proper approach to moral theory:

A consequence of the connection thus established between theory and experience in ethics is that the attempt to develop an adequate moral theory must of necessity be a moral undertaking itself. One hears it often said that the function of the moral philosopher is simply theoretical, that his aim is merely and solely to understand the facts of the moral life, or that his task is merely and solely to bring the deliverances of the so-called moral consciousness into logical, methodical coherence. Such a remark, however, can be made only by one who remains distant from what he is talking about, looking in another direction. One cannot theorize significantly about the moral aspects of friendship, for example, unless one is able to distinguish between, say, friendship based on utility and friendship based on love and to perceive that sacrifices which would be right in the latter would be wrong in the former. But once this is perceived by the theorizer it is perceived by him. And since he is a human being, he cannot avoid its impact upon his moral vision and behavior. He requires the moral insight in order to be a moral theorist, and the adequacy of his moral theorizing will depend upon that of his insight. Hence being moral must grow with thinking about morals, to the extent at least that moral insight has an effect upon moral character. Seen in this light, it is an essential part of moral theorizing that the thinker himself aspire constantly toward fuller and deeper moral vision. And since moral vision is significantly dependent upon moral character (for vice tends to blind us, and the passions that work against the right tend also to work against perception of the right), he cannot avoid the constant struggle to achieve moral perfection in himself. It follows then that while one may make a verbal or logical distinction between theorizing about morals and committing one's self to moral values, the two cannot be separated in fact. Indeed the history of ethical theory shows that any moral philosopher worth his salt—Socrates, Plato, Aristotle, Augustine, Aquinas, Spinoza, Hegel, Dewey—has always taken it upon himself, as an inescapable obligation, to reveal moral values, yes to preach them, to the utmost extent of his vision. (33:286)

10. Hofstadter speaks of the seriousness of moral philosophy:

All this shows that moral philosophy is a more serious undertaking than science, on the one hand, which abstracts as far as possible from human commitment, and art, on the other, in which (except when the artist or spectator can no longer prevent himself from exercising moral judgment) we are given the realization of life-forms without needing to assume the responsibility of estimating their values as such or of choosing them for ourselves. Indeed, moral philosophy, if we consider it adequately so as to include all forms of moral vision, is the only really serious mode of theorizing open to man. (33:286, 287)

11. John Laird on an adequate apprehension of the universe:

The pure in heart may not have greater sagacity concerning natural laws than other people, and yet may have much clearer insight than other people into the character of men and, in general, into what we describe as spiritual values. Furthermore, it is a question of perspective how far what we commonly call scientific insight should dominate our thoughts in this connection, and how far human, moral, esthetic, and theological insight should enter. It may well be maintained, although, I dare say, not without some moralistic pride, that an adequate and synoptic apprehension of the general character of the universe will never arise and will never be able to put central things in the center without very definite and very persistent moral preparation. (46:497, 498)

12. Price's views on the nature of questions which ought to be asked:

To use another analogy, we shall have made its rules so rigid that it becomes a strait-jacket, and prevents us even from asking questions which ought to be asked and from understanding the non-professional outsider who (in a confused way, very likely) is trying to ask them. Has it not happened sometimes that an important question was first asked by poets and religious teachers and other unphilosophical persons, who were blissfully ignorant of the terminological rules which the philosophers of their day had laid down? "Nonsense! Nonsense!" says the professional philosopher, when he is told of the question these people have asked. But his successors a generation or two later may call it unconscious wisdom or untutored insight; and having altered the terminological rules so as to make the question a permissible one, they may spend their professional lives in looking for the answer. In that case the philosopher who said "Nonsense!"

will appear a little ridiculous. Let us take care that this does not happen to ourselves, and let us not allow our zeal for "tightening up language" to run away with us. Even though we allow for the distinction between analytic clarity and synoptic clarity, it may still be true that clarity is not enough. (81:30, 31).

13. Hepburn concerning contemporary British moral philosophy:

Most recent British moral philosophy has been dominated by the "rule-obedience" model: moral judgment as the endorsing of principles, commitment to universalisable policies. There have been lately, however, some reminders that, whether or not rule-obedience may be the most satisfactory analysis of moral language, very different models are quite often in fact held by morally sensitive people—by those, for instance, who see moral endeavour as the realising of a pattern of life or the following out of a pilgrimage. Contemporary ethical writing certainly says little or nothing about whether such models are logically confused and benighted, or are witnessing to a philosophically neglected, but logically legitimate, way of viewing morality.

One can, of course, see reasons for the neglect. The language of "resolutions", "decisions of principle" is compatible with no-ghost-in-the-machine; but it is not so plain that we could work out the other models without reference to the spectral landscape of an "inner life". Secondly, the analysis of myth, parable, pilgrimage would involve considering language with far higher descriptive content than those terms (notably "good" and "ought") which have been the focus of recent study. More seriously, many people who speak the language of "bringing into being a pattern in one's life", speak of the pattern or pilgrimage not only as relevant to the question "what shall I do?" but also to those very embarrassing questions—"what does my life add up to?" "what is its meaning?" "is it coherent, integrated, or formless, chaotic?" "have I maintained initiative, been successfully creative; or has life gone past in uncreative passivity?" What can be said about these alarming violations of that jealously guarded ethics-aesthetics frontier? Can the philosopher of language address himself to such utterances without forfeiting all precision? Or, more to the point—is the language itself logically confused, merely picturesque or rhetorical? (26:14, 15)

141

14. Hofstadter on moral experience:

If we are to understand the moral dimension of human experience, it is necessary for us to keep that experience itself constantly in view. Moral theory which neglects moral experiences would be as absurd as aesthetic theory which overlooks aesthetic experiences or physical theory which flouts experimental data.

So obvious a caution would be superfluous were it not for the fact that there are ethical theorists who constantly violate it. Those who see in the rightness of an action nothing but conduciveness to good or to satisfaction, for instance, immediately betray a proneness to formulate their view in complete disregard of the most direct and primary experience of human acts in their moral aspect. It is morally right to respect nobility of character. Yet the rightness of the act of respect is, as such, independent of any good that may result from it.

There is therefore the closest possible tie between the having of moral experience (whether in actuality or in imagination, for no man can actually experience everything) and the ability to philosophize about morality. The morally immature are not fit students of ethics. (33:284)

15. T. E. Hill corroborates the need of considering particular ethical data as having significant bearing upon ethical theory.

Other problems of ethical theory [that is, along with the basic problems of the meaning of right and good, and the added, but distinct, problem of what makes these terms applicable] include those of the nature of the subjects of moral judgments, the character of moral standards, the objectivity or relativity of moral judgments, the nature of moral knowledge, the character of moral responsibility and merit, and perhaps those of moral motivation and freedom. Questions as to whether or not particular kinds of objects or acts are good or right belong more to applied ethics than to ethical theory, but they nevertheless have a significant bearing upon ethical theory in that in part ethical theories have to be tested by their capacity to sustain particular judgments of moral experience. (27:4)

Hill also claims that the Realistic Value theory is the best, but even so, it must deal directly with moral experience:

With the Process theories, a comprehensive version of the Realistic Value theory would, without confusing fact and value, insist that the search for the means of attaining value is as important a part of practical ethics as the discovery of value and that morality must constantly adapt its judgments to the factual processes of evolution and of economic, social, and cultural development.

The special merit of the Realistic Value theory lies on the one hand in its superior ability to interpret coherently our actual moral experience and on the other hand in its capacity to express in its own terms the best insights of the other theories. (27:354)

16. Bergson's comments on the consideration of action in moral philosophy:

Note: The following comments are Bergson's replies to questions put to him by Dr. Raymond F. Piper during the latter's visit at Bergson's home on February 19, 1921. They are still of more than historical interest.

W. H. Werkmeister

For a number of years I have been reflecting on the problem of moral values, and I am still reflecting on it. Modern philosophers have treated this problem with singular inadequacy. I really know of no modern thinker who gives a satisfactory answer to the question as to what one should do to find the good. Descartes and his successors certainly do not offer a practical solution; and even Kant has given us nothing definite. Try to apply Kant's universal rule to any of the particular problems of life which may face you, and you will find difficulty in finding guidance in his rule. I think that in modern French philosophy there is only one man who has said something suggestive on this question: Renouvier, in his book *Science de la Morale*. He really attacks the question of the practical problems of life.

I have found as yet no answer to the question as to what are the constituents of the highest good in life. I am searching. I have come to believe, however, that it cannot be contained or represented in a single formula. I think one must seek it by describing a multitude of experiences of great variety. When these are combined in one's life in a certain way, one may find the good life in this variegated whole.

I think that any philosophic truth can be expressed so

that the people, the average man, can understand it. But this expression is often difficult. It is seldom the first form that comes to mind. One usually puts truth in abstract form. One must be complete master of his subject and work long to succeed in presenting his ideas in popular form, and this presentation is likely to be long. (6:179, 180)

17. Bergson on certain inadequacies of the speculative function of the mind:

Our admiration for the speculative function of the mind may be great; but when philosophers maintain that it should be sufficient to silence selfishness and passion, they prove to us—and this is a matter for congratulation—that they have never heard the voice of the one or the other very loud within themselves. So much for a morality claiming as its basis reason in the guise of pure form, without matter. (7:87)

18. Hill on moral action and ideology:

It [moral philosophy] dare not keep its counsel to itself when the world is going to ruin. Ethical theories lie at the roots of prevailing ideologies, and the application of insights into moral meanings to present issues can help to resolve current confusion. Other disciplines have not been willing to take on moral issues alone. Philosophy has always been ready to inquire into basic questions not covered by the sciences, and moral philosophy must in full cooperation with the social sciences and the humanities actively lend its aid to the intelligent search for solutions of the crucial problems of our day. Refusing to quibble about boundaries of disciplines, it must acquire the generous spirit, as well as the rigor, of that love of wisdom which is philosophy. The reflex advantages of its excursions into practical ethics upon its own distinctive work will obviously be great; for the living endeavor to contribute to practical moral insights cannot but help to clarify moral meanings in the minds of those who make the endeavor, and, indeed, it is difficult to see how anyone can successfully do the work of moral philosophy without acquiring some of the firsthand data that are produced in the immediate effort to resolve practical issues.

In addition to performing its special theoretical tasks and aiding in the collection of moral data, the moral philosophy of our day must concern itself with the problems of practical morality at least to the extent of helping to mark out the broad outlines of values and duties and to indicate the principal motives for achieving the good and the right.

Contrary to the beliefs of many contemporary moralists, even ideally moral philosophy is not and cannot be merely an isolated theoretical discipline which serves no practical purpose. Rather, while it should never be diverted from inflexible pursuit of truth by pressure of practical issues, it is in the end an extension, in terms of the search for meanings, of man's practical endeavor to achieve the right and the good; and failure to accept its practical responsibilities would be a betrayal of the ultimate sources of its inspiration. Besides, whatever may be the case in ideal circumstances, the present situation involves radical conflicts of "isms" and ideologies that threaten to tear civilization into shreds; and while moral philosophy does not itself have the answers it does have keys to mutual understanding at many points. (27:358, 359)

19. A relationship does not have to be a primary relationship in order to be absolutely essential. We all remember the proverbial battle that was lost for the want of a horseshoe nail. Much contemporary moral philosophy has falsified its basic concepts by treating them as if their relationships had no effect upon their essence. Since morality deals only with human decision and its underlying concepts, it is as impossible to know the right, unrelated to action, as it is for human beings to be human unrelated to action. Moral philosophy has tended to neglect the essentially human gestalt and has in many areas become somewhat of a game of philosophers where it is difficult to feel blame for a wrong or foolish move. Much moral philosophy is now on this level, where the wrong statement on a moral level would be no more blameworthy than a wrong move in chess; this is one reason why the relationship to action is so unimportant to them. Moral philosophy is to many contemporary thinkers about the same as a mathematician's game playing with non-euclidian systems, but they forget that the moral game man plays is for keeps in a way that the mathematical game is not. The moral game does not wait for man the way other theoretical endeavors do.

The other point of confusion turns around a false concept of the nature of action. In the moral realm the concept of action includes decisions as well as any other type of the more obvious actions that are more easily perceived by the five senses. Because philosophers can think in terms of scientific, mathematical, or logical concepts that do not necessarily involve the decision procedure (or can they?) , many of them have assumed that this non-committal attitude can just as easily be transferred to moral conceptualizing. The assumption is that all theorizing should follow the methodology of science, mathematics, and logic. It has in fact been very instructive for philosophy to try this methodology in the moral realm; however, it is just as essential to know where scientific methodology does not apply as to know where it does. It is possible that the scientific methodologies could learn as much from a moral methodology of decision making (a form of action) as moral philosophy can learn from scientific methodology.

20. Price on the need of a unified conceptual scheme:

> Let us now return to the needs of the consumer. What he is alleged to need is a unified conceptual scheme of the sort I have been trying to describe. And I think it is true that he does need it. When the ordinary educated man speaks of "a philosophy," it is a conceptual scheme of this kind which he has in mind. Such a scheme, he thinks, will provide him with the wisdom which philosophers are traditionally supposed to supply. He needs, as it were, a map of the universe so far as our empirical information has disclosed it; and not a map of the physical world only, but one which makes room for all the known aspects of the universe, physical, spiritual, and whatever others there may be. He needs it nowadays more than ever, since for good reasons or bad the Christian metaphysical scheme has lost its hold over him; and Science does not give him what he wants either, since he feels (in my opinion rightly) that there are a number of very important questions on which Science has nothing to say. And he complains that just when his need is greatest, the philosophers are refusing to satisfy it. The prevalence of the purely clarificatory conception of Philosophy prevents them from even making the attempt. (81:27, 28)

21. Price on making things comprehensible:

> It would seem then that the complaint "clarity is not enough" is in one important respect justified, in so far as the

contemporary clarifying philosophers have neglected speculative Metaphysics, which is one of the things which philosophers are traditionally paid to know about. They have neglected it, not of course through mere laziness or inadvertence, but on principle, because they have thought that the speculative metaphysician is trying to do something which is from the nature of the case impossible: namely, to establish conclusions about matters of fact by means of purely *a priori* premises. But if I am right, that is not what he is trying to do, except in occasional moments of aberration. He is trying to do something much less extravagant and much more important: to produce a unified conceptual scheme under which all the known types of empirical fact may be systematically arranged. And there is nothing in this enterprise which even the most sensitive philosophical conscience need object to.

And the speculative metaphysician, at least as I have conceived him, could even accept the dictum that "Philosophy gives us no new knowledge, but only makes clear to us what we already know." For certainly it is not his function to give us new information about matters of fact, but rather to devise a conceptual scheme which brings out certain systematic relationships between the matters of fact we know already—including those queer and puzzling ones about which we know only a little. His job is to make things comprehensible, not to establish what things are. In short, is there not such a thing as synoptic clarity, as well as analytical clarity? And if we are careful to remember that the word "clarity" covers both of them, could we not conclude that clarity is enough after all? (81:28, 29)

22. Hill on the current confusion in contemporary ethical theories:

Such a time is our own. The older structures of political and economic order are crumbling and even the long secure anchors of personal morality are losing their hold. The stability that once marked national, racial, and class organizations has been lost. The events which led to two gigantic wars, together with the shocking callousness that accompanied them and the cynicism that has characterized a large part of the attempts to achieve adjustments after them, have unveiled radical conflicts in the mores and in such ideals as immediately control conduct. It is no wonder then that the current confusion in contemporary ethical theories is tragically costly. Not

147

only is moral philosophy in its present state unable to relieve the practical tension of our day, it often contributes to it, furnishing excuses for lack of principle in the contending parties and giving them weapons of ideological warfare. 27:2)

When one places this confusion in ethics against the background of imminent danger of destruction into which scientific advance has plunged civilization, the overwhelming conviction can scarcely be avoided that some new synthesis in moral philosophy must at all cost be sought, not to be sure as *the* way out but as a very necessary part of *a* way out. (27:33)

23. In this century, philosophers, excepting a few like Bergson, have shown considerable and widespread insensitivity to the issue of the proper balance between moral norms and their practical application and the relation of both of these to moral *dynamic*. Moral *dynamic* is both the cause and the effect of the proper balance of moral norms and moral action, of knowledge and belief, and of intellect and will. They have a circular relation in the sense that dynamic morality is begotten by this balance and then in turn the empirical forms of dynamic morality found in the moral geniuses of history serve to judge the balance of a moral system through calling for an equal amount of dynamic effectiveness.

24. The fact that the most highly developed complexus of justified beliefs is to be found within the framework of a moral ideology is merely a descriptive fact of current conditions. Moral philosophy should be teaching moral ideology about the creative role of justified belief; however, since moral philosophy has of late chosen to be unconcerned with belief, we have the strange situation where ideology must teach moral philosophy about belief in somewhat the same sense that science keeps philosophy abreast of empirical facts.

25. A moral ideology can remain moral only when it does not push some sectional point-of-view. Its moral norms must be considered to be universal and formal in the same sense that Kant held the moral law to be. A moral ideology, however, also possesses a form of *dynamic* which draws much like the supreme value of an axiological ethical system. It never uses force to push the human will. For example, a moral ideologist would lack something essen-

148

tial if he did not know how to inspire other people to follow their own highest value or to activate their own deepest commitment to a universal moral norm.

26. A definition of knowledge by C. I. Lewis under the title of "Terminating Judgments and Objective Beliefs":

> The existence of a thing, the occurrence of an objective event, or any other objective state of affairs, is knowable only as it is verifiable or confirmable. And such objective facts can be verified, or confirmed as probable, only by presentations of sense. Thus all empirical knowledge is vested, ultimately, in the awareness of what is given and the prediction of certain passages of further experience as something which will be given or could be given. It is such predictions of possible direct experience which we have called terminating judgments; and the central importance of these for all empirical knowledge will be obvious. (51:203)

27. Socrates referred to this type of cognition as 'knowledge' in that it was a definite part of knowing one's self. Contemporary epistemology would have to class these conviction-beliefs as 'faith.' The basic question at issue here is whether philosophers relate this type of cognition to knowledge in due respect for its moral importance; what they call it is not so important.

28. Spinoza's ethic is a classic example of a moral system that was born dead and impractical because of its total subservience to the methodology of geometry. Kant even claims that its dogmatic rigor of proof leads to such extremes as fanaticism. (39:302n)

29. That is, Locke might have seen the world through the lens of dogmatic scholasticism had he not continued to develop Descartes' stress upon methodology; or he might have seen the same world, through an excessive stress on method, in the complete scepticism of subjectivism had he not allowed his moral common sense to retain certain subject matter necessary for doing one's duty.

30. Kant on the primacy of practical reason:

> But far more important is the need of reason in its practical use, because here the need is unconditional; here we are compelled to presuppose the existence of God not just if we wish

to judge but because we must judge, for the pure practical use of reason consists only in the prescription of moral laws. They all lead to the idea of the highest good that is possible in the world so far as it is possible only through freedom, i.e., morality. And, on the other hand, they lead to something which does not depend merely on freedom but also on nature, namely, the greatest happiness so far as it is proportioned according to morality. Reason needs to assume such an independent highest good, and for its sake it needs also to assume a supreme intelligence as the highest independent good. It does not make these assumptions in order to derive obligatory respect for moral laws or incentives to their observance from the assumptions, for the laws would have no moral worth if their motive were derived from anything except the law alone, which is apodictically certain in itself. It needs to assume them only in order to give objective reality to the concept of the highest good, i.e., in order to prevent the highest good, and, consequently, all morality, from being regarded as a mere ideal, which would be the case if the highest good, the idea of which inseparably accompanies morality, never existed. 39:298, 299)

31. Kant describes the relation of reason to belief as follows:

To make use of one's own reason means nothing more than to ask one's self, with regard to everything that is to be assumed, whether he finds it practicable to make the ground of the assumption or the rule which follows from the assumption a universal principle of the use of his reason. This test can be applied to himself by each person; and by this test he will soon see superstition and fanaticism disappear even if he is far from possessing the knowledge requisite to a refutation of either on objective grounds. (39:305n)

32. I maintain that the clarification of the nature of belief is a key point in clarifying the relation between intellect and will because belief is the co-working of both. Unless moral philosophy deals with both, it will sell the subject short of its true scope. The idea of deciding is very essential to moral philosophy and this factor has an indispensable link to belief as well as knowledge. Moral thinking is essentially making decisions about the corrigible future, and this involves belief even though it may be a justified belief based on one's knowledge of past experiences. We cannot

help deciding because the very avoidance of it is itself a decision not to decide or to put it off (52:5, 9, 13, 15, 86). Hence, since deciding about the corrigible future always involves belief, we cannot avoid believing, regardless of what other names we may call it (51:206).

33. Northrop offers this definition of an ideology:

> A normative social theory, when its assumptions are made explicit, defines an ideology or in other words a possible moral and social philosophy. (73:424)

34. These reactions have largely been the result of very arbitrary usage of the word 'ideology' as found in writings like K. Mannheim's *Ideology and Utopia*. This confusion about meaning is common in sociological writings.

35. Few things have caused humanity more confusion than some of the ideologies. These are present facts and they cannot be corrected or re-channeled by more confusion. It is as foolish to ignore ideology as it is to ignore a flood because we may not like it. The best thing is to re-channel it where possible. There is no high-ground on which to escape its effects.

We need not think that ideology is against good philosophy. Ideology is as neutral as belief in regard to philosophy. When belief is given a chance, it gives a *dynamic* that mere fact cannot give because it may go where fact cannot go. The *dynamic* may be good or bad. Belief is unavoidable, but we can control our motives. Likewise ideology is here to stay, since pure reason fell; and it is a *dynamic* that is corrigible when we can find the secret of changing men's motives in the self-applied sense. Hence the question is not whether we like ideology, but what we do with it in a directive manner.

There is no real opposition between ideology and science. The real opposition, however, is prevalent between ideology versus scientism, ideologism versus science, ideologism versus scientism. Ideologism is ideology parading as a science in its presuppositions and final goals. Scientism is the parading of presuppositions as science, which are really ideological factors. Scientism is bad ideology and *not* science. Ideologism is pseudo science and bad ideology.

36. Northrop on ideology and free inquiry:

Why, in the face of this obvious fact, are past and present efforts at international collaboration so disheartening? This question brings us to the second fact necessary to the understanding of the contemporary world. This fact is the inescapably ideological character of its domestic and international problems.

Put very briefly, what this means is that different people and nations have different and conflicting ideals. The economic, political, and moral principles which one people or nation uses to order its business and political life and its legal institutions are not those of another. Hence, frequently what one nation or people regards as good, another nation or people deems to be evil. The Soviet Russians with their Marxist economic and political philosophy and the French and Anglo-Americans with their different philosophy deriving in great part from John Locke, Hume, Bentham, the French Encyclopaedists, and Jevons constitute one instance. The Latin-Americans with their conception of moral freedom as essentially psychological and emotional—a matter of passion rather than of reason—and the Anglo-Americans with their concept of freedom as essentially political in character are another example.

It is difficult to regard anything as much more important. In an atomic age we either understand and transcend the different ideologies of the world or we perish.

One point must be added. We are living in a world in which the ideology of one of its two major powers is that of the Marxist philosophy. It is a basic tenet of Marxism that ideas and ideals are not merely impotent but also evil unless they are embodied in matter and in the might of force. Such is the import of their designation of their philosophy as dialectical materialism. It is imperative therefore if free inquiry is to be allowed the chance and the time to understand the diverse ideologies of the world and to construct out of them the truly world ideology necessary to define the common principles for settling international disputes by recourse to law rather than to force, that the non-communist ideologies of the world be implemented with all the matter and might possible. This must be done not with the suicidal aim of deciding the issue by force but with the peaceful purpose of throwing the world into the power-politics and ideological equilibrium necessary to give free inquiry the time to work out its constructive solution of the problem. Otherwise free inquiry will not have its chance. (76:no page numbers)

37. Northrop on the need of precise ideological knowledge of dialectical materialism:

> Without precise ideological knowledge of what dialectical and historical materialism means, statesmen, whether they be Socialistic liberals, Quaker or Gandhian pacifistic neutralists, publicity-hungry fanatical McCarthys, oversmiling or over-grim generals or power politicians, are like love-sick girls wandering about blindfold picking petals off daisies in a field of booby traps fastened to atomic bombs. (75:244)

38. The communists tried this and still ended up with 'ideas' as their basic tools and weapons in spite of their "materialism."

39. I am not discussing the multitude of historical meanings of the word 'idea,' which is exemplified by the number of columns it covers in the *Oxford Dictionary;* my interest is only in those concepts of the nature of an idea that have been foundational and causal in the evolution of ideology as a fact and its necessary definitional elements. The closest dictionary meaning of 'idea' foundational to 'ideology' is the *Oxford Dictionary's* tenth usage, attributed to Descartes and Locke, in which it describes the word 'idea' as:

> Whatever is in the mind and directly present to cognitive consciousness; that which one thinks, feels, or fancies; the immediate object of thought or mental perception.

Another useful definition is found in Baldwin's *Dictionary of Philosophy and Psychology* which refers to 'idea' in a similar way as:

> The reproduction, with a more or less adequate *Image* of an object not actually present to the senses.

I am not trying to examine the full definition of 'idea' itself or even Descartes' or Locke's complete conceptions of the nature of 'idea'; my inquiry concerns only their conception of 'idea' which had some direct or indirect philosophical effect upon the development of later ideological philosophy as the referent and cause of the word 'ideology' which this chapter is discussing. (For fuller treatment of 'ideology' see Lichtheim. "The Concept of Ideology." *History and Theory,* Vol. IV, No. 2, 1965, 164-95.)

40. Leibniz criticized these criteria of clearness and distinctness on the basis that they were not logical but psychological precepts, giving them only subjective value (4:63), and Locke ultimately brought Descartes' dualism face to face with the fact that it implied that truth is in the last analysis the evidences of one's own mind.

41. Lerner makes an important observation concerning democracy that certain intellectualistic approaches have avoided. In my opinion this avoidance results from rationalism and scientism. Lerner says,

> For some time we have believed that there was a sharp difference between nations with "ideologies" enforced by state power and those in which the state was ostensibly neutral and allowed a competition of ideas. Several things have happened to bridge this sense of difference. One is that we have come more and more to view democracy as an ideology. (50:8)

42. This radical empiricism was most consistently formulated on a philosophical level in the 18th century by Condillac, who gained his own inspiration from Locke's "new way of ideas" in the *Essay Concerning the Human Understanding* and seized upon the sensationistic side of Locke's claim that "experience" is the origin of all ideas (*Essay,* Bk. II, Ch. I, Sec. 3) for use as an ideological dogma.

Following Condillac's example, the leaders of the French Revolution adopted a modification of Locke's doctrine of ideas, but only after making their own materialistic alterations. On this basis they used their new concepts of the nature of ideas as tools and weapons in order to combat the authoritative political and religious dogmas which had been used by the *ancien regime* to maintain control.

Even though Locke was the source of inspiration to Condillac and his followers, those men were not so wary as Locke about making great metaphysical jumps to their own conclusions concerning the nature of ideas. The "empiricism" of these French sensationistic thinkers is highly charged with the metaphysics of reductionistic, materialistic naturalism, through which they have shown their greatest insensitivity to the well-balanced and careful approach of Locke.

43. In *The Programme of the Communist International,* we see a good example of the positive use of 'ideology' stating the means of ideological influence:

Means of Ideological Influence

(a) The nationalisation of printing plans.

(b) The monopoly of newspapers and book-publishing.

(c) The nationalisation of big cinema enterprises, theatres, etc.

(d) The utilization of the nationalised means of "intellectual production" for the most extensive political and general education of the toilers and for the building up of a new socialist culture on a proletarian class basis. (12:999)

44. Khrushchev says,

(We must work for) the purity of Marxist-Leninist teaching. . . . Ideology is our strongest weapon. (9:125)

45. This definition is accurate as far as it goes, except that it leaves out the element of *dynamic* which is common to the most developed ideologies and which will be described in chapter 4 in relation to the scientific (methodological) and ideational (philosophical or world-view) elements included in the definition above.

46. H. D. Aiken describes this progress toward the practical in the realm of ideas:

What is perhaps not so clearly understood is that the more foundational doctrines of the nineteenth-century philosophers are also broadly ideological in character. By a strange paradox, Immanuel Kant, who thought that he had sounded the death knell to speculative metaphysics, initiated a great metaphysical revival in the absolute idealism of Fichte and Hegel. Yet, as we shall presently see, theirs was a form of metaphysics undreamed of by earlier philosophers. The difference between the metaphysics of a Fichte and that of a Descartes or a Leibniz is not, however, a theoretical difference, but a difference in regard to the very point and meaning of metaphysical theses. Essentially it is a difference between a form of inquiry which seeks theoretical knowledge of the most pervasive traits of being, and one which seeks to establish the basic commitments involved in being a man, being a person, being rational, or being civilized. Metaphysics was regarded by Descartes, and before him by Aristotle, as continuous with the inquiries of the special sciences, differing from them only in scope and primacy. For Fichte, on the contrary, its concern and its method essentially are practical, not theoretical; what it yields is not descriptions of matters of fact, but "posits" or commitments that are essential to the conduct of life. (1:ix)

47.   The factors that make Marx an ideological philosopher are in general those that added a definite ideological content to his predecessors such as Fichte, Hegel, Feuerbach, and even Kant.

Kant's contribution to the foundations of ideological philosophy centers in his stress upon the importance of will. Aiken says,

> For anyone who accepts Kant's doctrine of "the two reasons," as it has been called, and who, like him, holds that the foundation of all practical reason lies in the will rather than in the intellect alone, a whole major domain of philosophical reflection is removed, at a single stroke, from the exclusive jurisdiction of the scientific method. Ethics, and whatever else resembles it in this respect, may still be, in an important sense, "rational"; but in that case reason itself can no longer be regarded as a purely theoretical faculty. Moreover, if, as Kant holds, the only legitimate theological or metaphysical convictions are those which are based, finally, upon the demands of the moral will, then two other crucially important branches of philosophical inquiry are also removed from the domain which, however, liberally construed, may be called "science." In this historically important part of Kant's philosophy, one can, in short, see philosophy itself gradually shifting from the status of super-science to that of ideology. What is crucially significant, however, is that Kant himself can at once acknowledge this move in the case of ethics and still insist that it is a form of rational activity. (1:38, 39)

Marx's attitude concerning ideology as a fact may be epitomized in his famous saying, "philosophers have only interpreted the world

156

differently, the point is, to change it" (66:199). This point of view, which is not the generally accepted one in traditional philosophy, is basically that of an ideologist. Almost everything he wrote is generally consistent with this attitude or ideal of changing the process of history. Thus, the element of will, which seems to be a very dominant and necessary factor in all of the prominent world ideologies, begins to play a crucial role within the Marxian scheme in the form of practical purpose, even if it is not admitted to be such. Marx disguises this by such terms as "the inevitable" or "the dialectic," or other words which make his motives and those of his followers seem to be something more philosophically noble.

48. Blakeley claims, with apparent justification, that contemporary Soviet goals are essentially emotional constructions:

> Thus, we have seen that contemporary Soviet philosophy, as the theory of Communism, involves a belief in a future state of happiness for mankind, the "Communist destiny". This teleology is embodied in an organization which is universal because it is open to anyone who believes in the goal. And it is through this teleologically dynamic organization of believers that the results of the so-called "socialist construction" are said to be achieved. But this "heaven" is a natural, earthly state, where the progress is measured strictly in terms of Khrushchov's "material values". Further, we have seen that the "Communist destiny" is little more than a poor verbal expression of a purely emotional need and is not the rational expression of a clearly defined goal. Within this frame-of-reference of a striving toward a material goal with dogmatico-emotional means, contemporary Soviet philosophy finds its *raison d'etre* and we find, to some extent, an explanation of the paradoxical character of this philosophy which pretends to talk about a real, "material" world in the terms of modern science and which, in reality, ends up talking about a possible world in a sometimes quasi-mystic terminology and with a definitely theological method. (9:86)

49. As a morality of means, a distinction exists between strategy and tactics. Strategy is basic, and composes the unvarying plan-structure of the revolution; tactics are specific operations which vary with circumstances.

50. Among recent Russian expressions of this viewpoint are the following quotations found in Blakeley's appendices:

The fight for this new structure, the fight for the strengthening and completion of Communism, is the highest criterion of the moral conduct of people of the great epoch of the establishment of a new society. (9:136)

The ethical criterion of the socialist moral is the degree of correspondence of the education of the individual to the ideal of a fighter for socialism and Communism. The living embodiment of this ideal is the life and activity of K. Marx, F. Engels, V. I. Lenin and other great revolutionary Communists. (9:141)

The purpose of all the ideological activities of our Party and state is to develop the new traits of the Soviet people, to educate them in the spirit of Collectivism and industry, socialist internationalism and patriotism, the lofty ethical principles of the new society. (9:145)

51. Northrop on the different approaches to moral norms:

In this connection it is very interesting to note that the one branch of the United Nations into which the Soviet Union has not permitted its representatives to enter is the United Nations Educational, Scientific and Cultural Organization. They will not face and discuss objectively in UNESCO the ideological differences between the Communist and the free world. Nor will they collaborate or permit Russian scholars to collaborate in a scholarly, objective attempt to resolve these ideological differences . . .

The Soviet concept of international law and the content of their ideological conception of the moral and legal is such, therefore, that their own norms will not cause them to restrict to their own nation their war against what their ideology tells them is evil. Hence, a world community grounded in determinate legal rules implemented with the force necessary to make military aggression realistically unwise from the Communists' standpoint is absolutely essential. (75:254, 256)

52. V. G. Baskakov says,

Lenin and Stalin, working in the epoch of imperialism and the proletarian revolution creatively developed the ideas of Marx and Engels . . . (9:107)

L. G. Gorskova says:

The brilliant hero of the Russian and international workers' movement, V. I. Lenin, generalizing new historical

experience, elevated the teaching of Marx and Engels to a new
and higher level. (9:122)

53. Berdyaev on the Marxist-Leninist concept of freedom:

The philosophy of titanism presupposes a change in the
understanding of what freedom means. Marxist Leninism, or
the dialectic materialism of the period of proletarian revolution, gives a new meaning to freedom, and in fact, the communist meaning is very different from the usual meaning.
On this account Russian communists are honestly shocked and
indignant when they are told that there is no freedom in
Soviet Russia. Here is an instance. A Soviet young man went
to France for some months with the intention of then return-
ing to Soviet Russia. Towards the end of his stay he was asked
what impression France left upon him. He answered: "There
is no freedom in this country." The astonished retort was,
"What do you mean? France is the land of freedom. Everybody is free to think what he likes and to do what he likes;
it is with you that there is no freedom." Then the young man
expounded his idea of freeedom. In France there was no
freedom and the young man from the Soviet Union felt stifled
in it because it was impossible to change life in France, to
make a new life. The so-called freedom there was of a kind
which leaves everything unchanged; every day was like its
predecessor; you might turn out a government every week but
that altered nothing; and so the young man who came from
Russia was bored in France.

In Soviet communist Russia, on the other hand, there was
real freedom because any day might change the life of Russia,
and indeed the life of the whole world; it might re-make
everything. One day was not just like another. Every young
man felt himself a world-builder; the world had become
plastic and out of it new forms might be modelled. It was this
more than anything which acted on him like a charm. Everyone feels himself a partner in the common business, which
has a world-wide significance. Life is absorbed not in the
struggle for one's own personal existence but in the reconstruction of the world. So freedom is understood not as liberty of
choice, not as liberty to turn to the right or to the left, but
as the active changing of the world, as an act accomplished
not by the individual but the social man, after the choice has
been made. Liberty of choice divides and weakens the energies. Real constructive freedom comes after the choice has

been made and the man moves in the defined direction. Only that sort of freedom, freedom for the collective construction of life in the general direction of the communist party, is recognized in Soviet Russia; and it is precisely this freedom which is actual and revolutionary. French freedom is conservative; it hinders the social reconstruction of society and leads to everyone wanting to be left in peace and quiet.

Freedom, of course, must be understood also as creative energy, as the act which changes the world; but if freedom be understood exclusively in that way, and what takes place inwardly before that act, that realization of creative energy, is lost sight of, then the denial of freedom of conscience and freedom of thought is inevitable. And we can see that in the Russian communist realm freedom of conscience and thought is absolutely denied. There freedom applies exclusively to the collective not to the individual consciousness; the individual person has no freedom in relation to the social whole; he has no personal freedom and has no personal consciousness.

The interpretation by communism of the life of each man as the service of a supra-personal purpose, the service not of himself but of the great whole, is healthy, true and wholly in agreement with Christianity, but this true idea is distorted by the denial of the independent worth and value of each human person and of his spiritual freedom. (5:151, 152, 153)

54. This first category resembles the Western moralities because of its aim to build moral fiber within their own society. It is morality, however, only in the sense that it can have some reciprocal moral effect upon the ideology, otherwise it is ideology in a moral guise. The second category is obviously pure ideology with no possibility of being anything else.

55. This was well demonstrated in the North Korean prison camps where a significant number of "free" Americans, lacking a sense of wholistic responsibility, fell into moral degeneration.

56. The Soviet Institute of Philosophy says:

Creatively developing the deathless teaching of Marx and Engels on the revolutionary transformation of capitalist society into socialist society, Lenin and Stalin created a new and complete theory of Communist revolution, the theory of the possibility of the victory of socialism in one country. This theory gives an inexhaustible answer to the question on the ways and necessary conditions for the full victory of Communism throughout the entire world. (9:97)

57. Khrushchev says:

(We must work for) the purity of Marxist-Leninist teaching. . . . Ideology is our strongest weapon. (9:125)

It is necessary to analyse from every angle major processes taking place in the capitalist world, to expose bourgeois ideology, to fight for the purity of Marxist-Leninist theory. (9: 145)

Our line is clear: it is the line of war for the purity of the ideas of Marxism-Leninism, . . . (9:150)

It is necessary to fight constantly for the purity of Marxist-Leninist ideology, . . . (9:152)

58. B. A. Sabad says:

Bourgeois critics of Marxism try to avoid the serious analyses of the primary sources—the works of the classics of Marxism—because the works of the creators of scientific Communism, Marx, Engels, Lenin, are the most concrete models of that unity of theory and practice which is present in creative Marxism, and Dialectical and Historical Materialism are a firm and complete doctrine—powerful instrument of knowledge and of the revolutionary transformation of the world. (9:117)

59. Kierkegaard's book gives the essence of this concept in its English title, *Purity of Heart Is to Will One Thing.*

60. To date this superior ideology has appeared in the force of Moral Re-Armament. The *Congressional Record* mentions some interesting statements about it as an alternative ideology to Marxism, including statements by Konrad Adenauer.

In the "New York Journal American" (January 31, 1960) under the title "Adenauer Calls MRA World's Hope," Adenauer speaks of this ideology:

"At this time of confusion in Europe we need, and especially in divided Germany, an ideology that brings clarity and moral power into shaping international relations. A nation with an ideology is always on the offensive. A nation without an ideology is self-satisfied and dead . . .

161

"Dr. Frank Buchman, founder of Moral Re-Armament, is making a great contribution to international unity and to the establishment of social justice. A lasting memorial to his work is established in the hearts of mankind of this age. The way he has labored to establish relationships between men and nations on firm foundations of moral values will never be forgotten.

"Now is the time to work more strongly than ever for European unity through MRA. A Europe in which freedom and brotherhood should reign can only be created when nations are mutually conscious of their moral responsibility. MRA has given most valuable stimulation to the great work of uniting Europe. Unless this work is carried forward, peace in the world cannot be maintained.

"If all nations are to continue to live together, one of the most pressing tasks of our age is to overcome prejudices that exist between people, races, and nations. In this field MRA has made an important contribution.

"May it above all pass on the truth that the one real hope of nations living together in peace can only be found through a change in the human heart . . .

"We have seen the conclusion after some difficult negotiations of important international agreements. MRA has played an invisible but effective part in bridging differences of opinion between negotiating parties. It has kept before them the objective of peaceful agreement in search for common good which is the true purpose of human life.

"Begin with yourself—that, in my opinion, is the basic challenge of MRA. May this challenge ring out far and wide across the whole world and into all nations."

The *Congressional Record* also includes an interesting comment from the Kremlin and from Gabriel Marcel:

"A Finnish visitor to the Kremlin was told that the greatest obstacle to the advance of communism was MRA.

"Gabriel Marcel, the noted French Catholic philosopher and author, writing in the Paris newspaper Figaro, said: 'One fact which proves the scope of Moral Re-Armament is that the men of the Kremlin are troubled about it. They make many broadcasts as a warning against a movement which is undermining the very foundations of the Communist ideology.' "

A description of this ideology by both Moral Re-Armament and Radio Moscow:

"Moral Re-Armament is a superior ideology, with a superior strategy, because it meets the needs of the whole man and because it is available for all men everywhere—non-Communist and Communist alike. It is far more than the answer to Communism. It is the revolutionary idea that is putting right what is wrong and producing for every nation the incorruptible and inspired leadership that alone can create a full and free life for every nation. Radio Moscow itself has said (January 1953):

" 'Moral Re-Armament is a global ideology with bridge-heads in every nation in its final phase of total expansion throughout the world. It has the power to capture radical revolutionary minds. It is contaminating the minds of the masses. It substitutes for the inevitable class war, the eternal struggle between good and evil.' " (102:21, 3)

The Marxist-Leninist evaluation of this ideology has been translated from "Kommunist," the Moscow organ which gives the Party Line inside the Soviet Union:

"Moral Re-Armament is certainly the most prominent association which aims to save Western civilization from Communism. It has staff headquarters in Europe, Asia and America. These people hold assemblies in Latin America and even organize Pan-African conferences. . . . The leaders of Moral Re-Armament claim it is superior to capitalism and Communism. . . . At a time when the morals of the bourgeois world are bankrupt, the prophets of Moral Re-Armament say that the world requires an ideology to satisfy the longing for absolute standards, an ideology able to move the hearts of the privileged as well as the under-privileged. . . . They train officers, philosophers, film directors and move with 200, 300, or 400 people in strength with up-to-date technical equipment, radio transmitters, libraries. . . . Not long ago they issued a call to Communists through full pages in the press. In this the Communists are challenged to take part in 'the greatest revolution of all time.' These people say the problem is neither Communism nor capitalism, but the necessity to change human nature to the roots. They puff themselves up with pride and even suggest to Marxists they should change and take up an ideology that is for everybody. This is really the most bold stroke that has come from these propagandists of reconciliation and forgiveness." (103:A21)

61. From the vantage point of an outsider, however, the principle of self-criticism is not universal in its application: basic strategy and philosophy are exempt, and, as far as it may be ascertained, the top leadership have seldom admitted any error as long as they have held personal power. Khrushchev did his best to extricate himself from his part in the crimes of Stalin against his own countrymen, and present leadership is disavowing itself of Khrushchev's blunders.

62. Iovcuk says:

> On the foundation of living and all-conquering Marxist-Leninist doctrine, creatively developed in the resolutions and documents and practice of the CPSU and other Marxist-Leninist parties, by means of a profound and systematic mastery of the entire richness of the ideas of Marxism-Leninism, by ceaseless control over the most important fields of knowledge collected by men and, above all, by means of active participation in Communist work, Soviet youth will be educated in the spirit of Communist consciousness and morality. (9:139)

V. S. Kruzkov says:

> Leninism is inseparable from Marxism, this is the one complete revolutionary doctrine of the international proletariat, called Marxism-Leninism. A revision of Marxism is a revision of Leninism and a revision of Leninism is a change in Marxism. The creative development of Marxism in the works of Lenin and after his death in the resolutions of the CPSU, in the collective works of our Party, of fellow Communist and workers' parties on the basis of new experience of international working and freedom movements and the experience of the construction of Communism and socialism in the countries of the world-wide socialist system, concretely demonstrate how to implement the Leninist principle of the inseparable unity of philosophy and politics. (9:139)
>
> The resolutions of the 20th and 21st Congress of the Communist Party of the Soviet Union are incomparably clear and persuasive models of the creative development of Marxist-Leninist philosophy. (9:139, 140)

164

63. In the following quotation, Paton shows how to detect Marxist scientism:

> The principal question before us is this. Does Marxist dialectic give a scientific account of nature and subsequently extract from this its moral and political ideals; or does it, on the contrary, pick and choose in nature precisely those phenomena which look as if they provide support for moral and political ideals independently formed? Wherever we find in a professedly scientific account the use of words like "important", "higher", "onward" and "upward", we may be sure that the author is not being scientific, but is on the contrary injecting his own moral ideals into his science. (79:311)

64. Hepburn on the element of art in man's remaking:

> I wish first of all to examine the claim, made by some (but by no means all) of those who see their lives in the way outlined above, that "man makes himself," that men may be considered as artists, their own lives the artefact. For here the aesthetic instrusion seems most extravagant, most liable to lead to cloudy nonsense. Granted, the metaphor of the artist is not wholly absurd—artist and artefact may be said to be one, when, for instance, a dancer performs a dance of his own devising; but something more precise is required than metaphor. I shall say, then, that "man makes himself" is partly often a rhetorical way of expressing the irreducibility of value-decisions to facts, and the revolt against any sort of "heteronomy of the will." (26:17)

65. New Testament Christianity has also had a definite plan for vice which has been to cut it out by its roots, to cure it through a transformation of human nature: society was to be given an impetus toward a new age by the change that came in men. Thus we see St. Paul using his cured vice of persecuting Christians as a lever to awaken others to the transforming power of God (Acts 22:1—11; 26:9—23). Transformed "vice" was an essential part of Paul's ideological plan against evil and spiritual ignorance.

66. For example, the present tactic of Russian communism is to use the West's and neutralists' "virtuous" desire for peace (meaning no shooting) as a tactical instrument to destroy the greater and more universal peace that comes from liberty based upon the right of responsible dissent (75:256).

67. The Marxist-Leninist's use of vice might demonstrate how a plan for vice, complementing a definition of virtue, equals more than a mere normative definition of virtue which neglects some pragmatic plan for vice within its overall scheme. Definitional virtue alone presumptuously assumes that man begins from morally objective grounds.

68. Just as Marxist-Leninists use their own virtues to help the revolution, they also use the vice of their enemies (84:92, 150, 156). But their most clever tactic of ideological moral strategy is their actual ability, through the totalness of their world-view, to pervert many of the virtues of their enemies that are of lesser ideological adroitness and stature. As a consequence of this tactic, we have entered a new era where the power of logic to move the human will in Western morality has met its match in the power of ideology. The comparison between the power to move the will of Western morality and that of Marxism-Leninism is essentially a comparison of rationalistic consistency in the case of the former versus totalistic, empiricistic dynamism in the case of the latter. Whereas Western philosophers have majored on logical rigor of the form of the thinking that corresponds to the moral act, the Marxist-Leninists have majored upon the dynamic and dialectical scope of moral action. Each has its own kind of logical consistency even though the point of consistency is diverse; consistency comes in the form of traditional logic among Westerners, whereas it appears among Marxist-Leninists as dialectical logic (which is really a form of ideology) moving consistently toward an ultimate goal.

Consistency alone does not constitute moral reality. Much of the perfection of exclusively formalistic ethics is a pseudo perfection that is consistent but unreal. (In the same way, Aristotle's final causes got by logic and analysis for centuries even though they had no reality for demonstrable knowledge in physics, in spite of their humanistic and cosmic significance.) Realizing this pragmatic unreality, the communists have come upon an important factor in the moral life of man and human history: abstract morality does not have the historic effectiveness of ideological morality. Ideologies are dynamic and eschatological; they are history-directing patterns toward, for instance, the Kingdom of God or the classless society; they concern not arm-chair or ivory tower discussion but the actual making of the history of individuals and nations. The ideologist is not *per se* against abstract excellence, but only that abstractness that lacks the empirical moral reality of an inclusion of, or a connection with, history-making *dynamic*. Whereas the Marxist-Leninists lack in the traditional logical rigor, they make up for it pragmatically (i.e. not in an intrinsically moral way but ideologically speaking) through their totality of scope through dialectical logic and the empirical use of the actual moral conditions of humanity.

69. The Marxist-Leninist concept of the 'right orientation':

> Marxism-Leninism is an integral and consistent dialectical materialist world outlook, and the theory of scientific Communism . . . This theory enables the Party to ascertain the laws governing social life, to find the right orientation in any situation, to understand the inner connection of events and the trend of their development. (86:748)

70. Moral ideologists have referred to these same three elements as (1) a passion, (2) a philosophy, and (3) a plan (14:13).

71. Hocking may add some light to my working definition of 'ideology' by way of negation in his claim that Christianity

> is not, and never can be, an ideology, specifying a program for world order with an economic and political as well as moral goal; yet there is not a corner of human life toward which it admits itself irrelevant (28:128)

Christianity is not an ideology if it is considered that its essence is "Christ in you" (Col. 1:27, R.S.V.) but it includes the animation of an ideology, and implies an ideology. "Christianity" as institutionalism is at best an ideology, and usually less. The factor of a personal God at the heart of the theistic religions keeps them from being merely an ideology; the personality of God cannot be reduced to an idea or a conceptual tool even though It produces ideas capable of ideological usage.

72. Laird on the need for passion in the search for truth:

> It is very common, and very perverse, to omit to distinguish between what is disinterested and what is uninterested. In reality, there is no incongruity in a "passion" for abstract

167

justice, or for intellectual candor; and there are very few eminent scientists and very few eminent jurists who do not possess this passion in a marked degree. No one, indeed, ever set about in seriousness to discover truth without having a passion for truth; . . .

Secondly it should be remarked that passion and emotion are not irrelevant to all beliefs. . . . emotion may be a prior condition for certain kinds of insight or penetrative beliefs. (46: 154, 155)

73. The best modern philosophical treatment on this subject is found in Rudolph Otto's *Idea of the Holy.*

74. Schoeck's indictment of scientism is as follows:

Moreover, scientistic interpretation of the study of man throws the scholarly grasp of human nature and its volitions open to ideological manipulations when least suspected. Quantities can be as subjective an argument as a stress on qualities. But most people are less aware of this fact. If the public or fellow scholars are unwilling, for prescientific, i.e., ideological reasons, to accept our arguments, statistical data and their expert manipulation will not convince them. Indeed, we can always startle our positivistic friends in the social sciences by asking them to name just one major policy decision or law that came about, against the popular and political preferences for it, on the strength of quantitative data. Can we recapture the proper—i.e., most fertile—balance between elements of measurement, of quality, and of form in the study of social man?

Over a number of years participants in this symposium, and others, have shown, in their individual publications, increasing concern with the harm done to the true study of man, especially as a social being, by a form of scientism that takes various disguises of strict scientificalness. It is not merely neopositivism, which, by the way, has been criticized by a number of able men; it is also more than a cult of quantification. Scientism implies a cynical world view—in the original meaning of the word: it is a doglike view of man, or shall we say ratlike? Man is best understood, so the scientistic expert holds, when seen from the level of a rodent eager to learn the ins and outs of a maze. He can be conditioned to put up with almost anything the few wise designers of the maze have mapped out for him . . .

Similarly, I am afraid, the arrival and pushing of quantitative methods in the social sciences corrupted young sociologists and social psychologists. They are so proud of the presumed power of statistical tools, of measurement of attitudes, for instance, that they never learn how to observe significant phenomena in their field of study. They learn all about "measuring" attitudes before they can tell one attitude from another by looking at a human being in social action.

This helplessness of our social scientists is shown, for instance, by their failure to come to grips with the phenomenon of aggression. Learned teams have tried to discover what makes human beings aggressive. They have studied international tensions, hostilities, frustrations, and other surface phenomena. It has hardly occurred to them to go beyond the terms "aggression" or "hostility." If they had been as open to such problems as were our students of man in the nineteenth century, it could not have escaped their attention that envy is a much more basic common denominator for various phenomena of "aggression" or "hostility" than "frustration," although a less flattering motive with which to excuse the perfidy of a Hitler or a Castro. The frustration theory nearly allows one to put the blame on the alleged frustrator; in the case of envy, this is a little more difficult.

W. T. Couch has made pertinent comments on this point: the developments we have come to call scientism are probably, in part, responsible for the facility with which social scientists circumvent crucial phenomena of human action that have traditionally formed a link between the empirical observation of man and normative philosophy. (89:ix, x, xiii, xiv)

75. Concerning reasonableness, Laird says,

It is true that no further reason can be given here. The ultimate analysis of moral experience in this matter is simply that the best does command, although its commands may not be obeyed. This is a dictate of the best to a creature responsive to values in so far as it appreciates them; and we cannot believe, I think, that this connection between the idea of value and the actions which may be guided by that idea, is simply psychological fact that happens to have a place in the constitution of the human species. On the contrary we believe it to be the implicate of insight and of right reason. (47:24)

76. Edmond Cahn gives a good analysis of the relationship of the passive to the active by the example of moral equality:

As passive equality pertains to the necessities of decent human subsistence in a democratic society, active equality pertains to the opportunities for personal improvement and advancement. As passive equality provides a floor, active equality invites men to raise themselves as far above the floor as their individual capacities permit. The ideal of active equality is particularly relevant during a period of social or economic transformation because it admonishes that the benefits arising from discovery, invention, and general progress shall be made available to all members of the community. In this way, as passive equality seeks to provide limits for men's fears, active equality seeks to remove limits from their hopes.

While America has usually been a follower in establishing public institutions of passive equality, it has characteristically led the world in championing the cause of active equality. (13:122, 123)

77. R. B. Braithwaite shows that man must act even on unverifiable beliefs as well as on empirical beliefs:

By emphasising the pragmatic and behaviouristic element common to all kinds of sincere belief, whether verifiable or unverifiable, I may have made it appear less shameful to hold unverifiable beliefs. Indeed by pointing out that changes of behaviour involved in unverifiable beliefs are, since they go along with changes in the springs of action, more radical than the mere adaptations which arise from ordinary empirical beliefs, I have exalted the former to a high place in the hierarchy of practical principles. I have given him, it is true, no guidance as to the choice of such principles; I have indicated that he must make the choice for himself. (10:19)

78. C. I. Lewis treats this assumption of science in its stabilizing role:

I recognize that my burden of proof in this matter is a heavy one. Belief in something meant by the "uniformity of nature" is, I think, as natural to us as belief in an absolute up and down, and is supported by many habits of thought which are fundamental and pervasive. And so far as I know, it has never up till now been questioned, except by those who willingly faced a skeptical alternative. In a sense, this belief is not to be questioned here, but, rather whether it has any alternative at all; the precise problem is, perhaps, just what is involved in the necessary "uniformity." (53:348, 349)

79. Iredell Jenkins' view of the significance of the conscience:

Conscience is the voice of man's total concerns—the agent of his participation in the human enterprise—and not the echo of some narrow system of values. (37:270)

80. A. C. Garnett on the advance of conscience:

For the purpose of our understanding of the development of conscience, however, the point of greatest importance is this: the recognition of the distinction between the law as it is and the law as it ought to be (and of a moral ideal too high to be made a law) is a distinct advance made by the ethical thought of civilized man over the vague moral assumptions and confusions of the primitive. And this advance, once achieved and maintained, opens the way for others. (23:34)

81. A. C. Garnett on a mature concern for the welfare of others:

The significant fact, therefore, which emerges from our study of the development of conscience, is this: that man's reflective analysis of his own moral nature discloses within him something that he can understand only as an inner demand that he concern himself impartially with the welfare of other human beings. And this discovery has been so startling and compelling to those who have made it that they have attributed it to something, indeed, that is more than human. (23:41)

82. A. C. Garnett on the realness of the conscience:

For the present it is not with this religious conclusion that we need to be concerned. If we would understand the moral nature of man, we must not too readily jump to the conclusion that in this religious interpretation of their experience the sages are right—or that they are wrong. The important thing is to recognize the nature of the experience and the method of thought and inquiry out of which these moral convictions have come. For such experience is not peculiar to the sages and prophets who first propound these new and higher moral ideals. If it were, then no one would listen to them. The prophets and sages win a following because what they say finds echoes in the breasts of their hearers. These latter find their own moral consciousness illuminated thereby. The ethical and religious literature produced by the prophets and sages becomes classical, and acquires the reputation of inspiration, because it says so well and clearly what the multitude also vaguely feel. To many of their hearers, the illumination of the moral consciousness thus induced is disturbing and unwelcome. They may stone or crucify the prophet in resentment. But those who come after them and reflect more calmly on the new moral ideal are won to respect it because it appeals to them as true. They then build the prophet's tomb, canonize his writings, and perhaps worship at his shrine.

No explanation of the moral phenomenon in history can be adequate unless it explains the phenomenon in this form. It is irrelevant to point out that few persons, if any, act consistently in accord with such high moral convictions. This only renders more remarkable and striking the fact that they have these convictions—for the fact that they do not act upon them means that wishful thinking would make them desire to get rid of such convictions if they could. Yet the uncomfortable convictions persist. It is also irrelevant to point out that many persons do not hold these convictions and declare that they have no such sense of obligation as is implied by them. The fact that such obligations are unwelcome is sufficient to explain why many persons should be psychically blind to them. The further fact that recognition of these duties or ideals has, historically, been a plant of slow growth, and has always faced opposition from those whose interests or prejudices are adversely affected, also explains why it is comparatively easy for many persons, even in our civilization, to reject them and deny any experience by which to justify them.

The opposition to these ideals, therefore, and the denial of their validity, does not lessen our problem. The fact to be explained is that moral conviction has, historically, taken this high and universalistic form, and that such conviction is widespread and is given almost universal lip service even where violated in practice; for this indicates that it is unwillingly recognized as right. Also to be explained is the manner in which such convictions have grown—by reflective analysis of the sense of obligation and value on the part of individuals deeply concerned with moral issues, and by the more or less reluctant recognition, on the part of those to whom the new concepts of obligation have been taught, that these insights are right. It is irrelevant for the critic to point out that the principles of love to one's neighbor and equality of rights are all too often violated by individual selfishness and group fanaticism. The fact of significance for an understanding of the moral nature of man is that his conscience, especially as manifest in the teaching of the religions he has accepted as civilization has given him leisure to think, has generally endorsed these principles. The fact that his inclinations so often lead him to violate or distort that conscience only makes its emergence and persistence the more remarkable. (23:41–43)

83. These two columns give the contrast between *eros* and *agape* as forms of love:

Eros	*Agape*
Eros is acquisitive desire and longing.	Agape is sacrificial giving.
Eros is an upward movement.	Agape comes down.
Eros is man's way to God.	Agape is God's way to man.
Eros is man's effort: it assumes that man's salvation is his own work.	Agape is God's grace: salvation is the work of Divine love.
Eros is egocentric love, a form of self-assertion of the highest, noblest, sublimest kind.	Agape is unselfish love, it "seeketh not its own," it gives itself away.
Eros seeks to gain its life, a life divine, immortalized.	Agape lives the life of God, therefore dares to "lose it."
Eros is the will to get and possess which depends on want and need.	Agape is freedom in giving, which depends on wealth and plenty.
Eros is primarily *man's* love; God is the *object* of Eros. Even when it is attributed to God, Eros is patterned on human love.	Agape is primarily *God's* love; "God *is* Agape." Even when it is attributed to man, Agape is patterned on Divine love.
Eros is determined by the quality, the beauty and worth, of its object; it is not spontaneous, but "evoked," "motivated."	Agape is sovereign in relation to its object, and is directed to both "the evil and the good"; it is spontaneous, "overflowing," "unmotivated."
Eros *recognises value* in its object —and loves it.	Agape loves—and *creates value* in its object.

For Nygren, Eros, and Agape are irreconcilable and stand as direct opposites. Of them he says:

> For Eros chief weight is undoubtedly given to self-love. Eros demands satisfaction for its own desire and longing. Hence it can find ample room also for love towards God, since God as the Highest Good is the satisfaction of every desire. It has less room, however, for neighbourly love. Indeed, it would be truer to say that the thought of neighbourly love is alien to the Eros-outlook, into which it was first introduced through a compromise with the Agape-outlook. When Eros-love is directed to a fellow-man, it is because he is regarded, not as a "neighbour," but as an object which participates in the Idea of the Beautiful, or in the higher world generally, and which can therefore be used as a means of ascent to that world. One form of love has absolutely no place at all in the scheme of Eros, and that is God's love.
>
> .   .   .   .
>
> Agape runs directly counter to all this. For Agape it is precisely God's love, God's Agape, that is both the criterion and the source of all that can be called Christian love. This Divine love, of which the distinctive feature is freedom in giving, has its direct continuation in Christian neighbourly love, which having received everything freely from God is prepared also to give freely. Here, therefore, we have no need to try to make room for neighbourly love, nor to find any external motivation for it. It is God's own Agape which seeks to make its way out into the world through the Christian as its channel. As regards love towards God, on the other hand, we can certainly not say that it has no place within the scheme of Agape, but we must say that its meaning is quite other than in the context of Eros. It has got rid of the egocentric, acquisitive character that is irreconcilable with the unreserved devotion of a man to God and his complete possession by God. . . . But one form of love has absolutely no place in the context of Agape motif, and that is self-love. (77:210, 218-19)

84. Ravines relates what Mao Tse-tung said to him about the central use of opportunism in Marxist-Leninist tactics:

> "The immense mass of our friends and enemies is made up of opportunists. You must get that through your head—complete opportunists . . .

"We are not even going to suggest that you should conduct a political campaign in favor of the dictators, or that you should hitch the party fortunes to the wagon of military victors. Not at all. On this point we must be very clear.

"There are social sectors, there are countries which have real party politics, a democratic life, real civil liberties. In such places one adopts the Popular Front, to attract the left-wingers and the leftist groups, good or bad, sincere or not. Tempt them, each through his particular weakness, as the devil tempts. You understand? Help them to get what they want; put pressure, first with offers, later with threats. Compromise them if you can, so that they can't get away. And this everyday, without respite, one after the other with as deep a psychological study of each as possible. That is the easiest to understand, isn't it?" (84:156)

85. Gordon Kaufman gives a good analysis of these absolutes:

Insofar as these standards and criteria are the farthest limit to which we can push our attempts to achieve validity, and insofar as we find we must judge everything else in terms of them, they are what T. Z. Lavine has called "functional absolutes." That is, they function in the cognitive process as absolutes, and we apprehend them as absolutes, but neither in our use of them nor in our apprehension of them may they be regarded as absolute metaphysical realities, for they are subject to criticism and change. Contrary to Lavine's views, however, the question of the metaphysical status of these "functional absolutes" [Y. H. Krikorian (ed.), *Naturalism and the Human Spirit,* pp. 197ff] cannot be ignored. Our willingness constantly to use them in the pursuit of truth, to criticize them in the name of truth, and finally to stake our existence on them implies a faith that they are somehow rooted in what is ultimately real, beyond all illusion. It is by this faith that the most radical doubter lives, and it is in this faith that the most radical doubt is ultimately justified (in the religious sense). Thus the very way in which we live by, use, and criticize our criteria—whatever may be the existential and psychological roots out of which they have grown—raises metaphysical questions about the nature of our world and ourselves as well as about the nature of the criteria, and these questions cannot be ignored. No matter how historically conditioned and relative are both our criteria of truth and all "truths" that we know, we have open to us no alternative but to live and act and think in terms of the norms impinging upon us and the "truth" accessible to us. We thus inevitably (if often unconsciously) premise our every action and thought on the conviction (perhaps unprovable, but nevertheless inescapable) that our knowledge somehow participates in that which transcends the relativities of our situation. (43:85, 86)

86. The problem of absolute moral standards is paralleled by C. I. Lewis's comment upon the problem of consistency:

The creature which is not driven by impulse but must sometimes make his own decisions, must also find it imperative to respect consistency—in concluding and believing, in purposing, and in doing. Principles of action (of decisions to do), like principles of thinking (of decisions as to fact, conclusions), are finally rooted in respect for consistency.

Decisions of action have their premises, as decisions of belief have their premises. Consistency concerns the relation between a decision and its premises, and, more widely, the relation of all accepted decisions—all convictions of justified believing and justified doing—among themselves. Complete consistency would be the complete integrity of a completely rational self.

A rule of decision is valid a priori if the repudiation of it would be self-contravening—a pragmatic contradiction. Such a non-repudiable principle is "pragmatically a priori." The broadest of imperatives, "Be consistent," exemplifies this matter. A decision without intent to adhere to it would not be a genuine decision. But one who should adopt the decision, "Disregard consistency," would be deciding to disregard his decisions as soon as made. And adherence to that decision would require that it be promptly disregarded. (54:100, 101n)

87. Kant speaks of reverence (in comparison with love) in this negative sense, upon which it becomes a stabilizing factor to the moral life. He says,

But LOVE must not be here understood to mean an emotion of complacency in the perfection of other people, there being no obligation to entertain feelings; but this love must be understood as the practical maxim of goodwill, issuing in beneficence as its result.

The same remark holds of the REVERENCE to be demonstrated towards others, which cannot be understood simply to mean, a feeling emerging from contrasting our own worth with that of another,—such as a child may feel for its parents, a pupil for his ward, or an inferior for his superior in rank,—but must be taken to mean, the practical maxim of circumscribing our own self-esteem, by the representation of the dignity of the humanity resident in the person of another; that is, A PRACTICAL REVERENCE.

This duty of the free reverence owed to other men is properly, negative only, viz. not to exalt ourselves above others. It is in this way analogous to the juridical duty "to do no wrong," and so might be taken for a strict and determinate obligation; but, regarded as a moral duty, and a branch of the offices of charity, it is a duty of indeterminate obligation.

The duty of loving my neighbor may be thus expressed,— that it is the duty of making my own the ends and interests of others, in so far as these ends are not immoral. The duty of reverencing my neighbour is expressed in the formula, to lower no man to be a bare means instrumental towards the attaining [of] my own ends, i.e. not to expect from any man that he should abase himself to be the footstool of my views. (41:293)

88. A. C. Garnett has defended this point admirably in "Relativism and Absolutism in Ethics." He says,

The thesis of this paper is that most of the confusion and disputation on the problem of relativism and absolutism in ethics is due to a failure to make a proper distinction between the right and the good. If this distinction is properly maintained, it will, I believe, be found that there is a general consensus of opinion on the major issues among nearly all moral philosophers and the great majority of civilized people. There also appears a happy solution from the standpoints of the disputants themselves, for the relativists are shown to be correct as to the nature of the good, while the absolutists can claim the honors on the question of the nature of the right. The good is relative; the right (We are speaking here, of course, of the "morally" right, i.e., right in the ethical sense of the term.) is absolute. (24:186)

89. Concerning moral principles, Paton says,

A moral principle is absolute—that is, it holds in all situations. A moral law, and still more a moral rule, is only one application of a moral principle and must also be relative to a special kind of situation. Thus even a law or rule may be called absolute in the sense of not being dependent on the likings or dislikings of the agent and of holding for all men in a like situation; but it is not absolute in the sense of holding for all situations whatsoever.

Only by making a distinction of this kind can we avoid an absurd rigidity which leads men—often through misunderstanding—to reject out of hand the doctrine that moral principles are absolute and universal. Such a distinction also compels a good man—and this too is wholesome—to recognize that his judgments about his duty in a particular situation are not infallible although he has to act as if they were. All he can claim is that they may be right or wrong, true or false (unless we confine truth and falsity to scientific statements). How such a claim can be tested is too large a question to examine here; but in doubtful cases we have to start from common beliefs and practices and criticize these in the light of our ultimate principles. In the end there may come a time for decision or experiment. It would be absurd to deny that even more principles can have their full meaning only in relation to a whole system of rights and duties. In this sense they may be enriched, expanded, and illuminated with a wider experience and with that deeper moral insight which can be attained only in action. We must always assume that we have made some way already; and each moral discovery may become, as it were, the instrument of further advance.

Belief in the absolute claims of duty does not prevent us from being tolerant or from recognizing both that our judgment is fallible and that the principles of morality have to be applied differently in different circumstances. But it does assume that there are ultimate moral principles by which a good man must judge and on which he is obliged to act. These principles may be difficult to formulate, difficult to apply, and still more difficult to justify; but they must nevertheless be presupposed in our moral judgments and moral actions, and without them there is no morality at all.

Moral principles bear a certain resemblance to the theoretical principles of synthesis discussed in Chapter XVIII, Sec. 4, or again—if something more familiar is wanted—to the principles of induction, without which there could be no science. All such principles (including the so-called Principle of Verification) have to be distinguished from generalizations about the way men in fact think and behave—most men think incompetently and behave badly. On the other hand, men may think and act on principles which they cannot clearly formulate; and it is only by principles, however, vaguely grasped, that they distinguish sound scientific thinking or good moral action from their opposites. Is it not partly an unreasoned intellectualistic prejudice that makes so many thinkers to-day boggle at moral principles even when they are prepared to swallow theoretical principles without a qualm? It is hard to see why moral principles should be regarded as less intelligible or less rational than are, for example, Mr. Russell's five postulates of scientific inference [in] his book on *Human Knowledge*.

In spite of their resemblance we should not forget the difference between moral and scientific principles; for moral principles are principles of action and not merely of thinking. This is the reason why moral judgments arouse stronger feelings—so much so that they are often thought to be founded on emotion. Moral judgment makes a claim, not merely for theoretical assent, but for practical co-operation as well; and the refusal of practical co-operation, still more an attempt at practical opposition, will arouse more passion than is found in our not always unemotional theoretical disputes. (79:297—299)

90. Belief cannot exist without will if it goes beyond the "given" (82:Ch. 1).

91. Paton shows this is a necessary linguistic distinction; however, we must not assume the reality of pure intellect as scientism often has done (79:61). (See Ap. 93.)

92. Mure on the ubiquity of will:

A moment's reflection makes this clear. Morality is practical, but the will operates in all activities whether their essence is practical or not. It is a commonplace that aesthetic, philosophical, and scientific activities are ruined if they are set to work under a moral directive, but this does not remove the moral obligation on a painter to quicken his vision and improve his art, on a philosopher to think straight, on a scientist not to falsify facts. Each of them has a moral duty to resist interference from outside his profession, but each soon enough finds his conscience working within it. It is the awareness of the good will as in this sense ubiquitous that the moral agent

179

first discovers his practical activity to be not simply finite, and that, I think, is the beginning of the religious consciousness. (71:222)

93: Schiller shows this rationalistic error of excluding the role of belief:

> [The rationalist account of belief as a purely intellectual matter is even intellectually defective.] It does not represent truly the procedure of human reason. It omits to record that our reason everywhere demands the stimulus of interest, the prospect of a desired end, intelligent choice in the selection of the means to that end, and persevering efforts to attain it. It cannot explain the function of faith in religion, and the role played in scientific knowing by postulates, hypotheses, fictions, interpretations, and other cognitive operations in which the first move seems to be with man.
>
> All belief is a more or less volitional affair, simply because it is an act of our total personality, and because a reason that is pure, a desire that is blind, and a will that is mere, are all fictitious abstractions. They explain nothing, because, how and why a man reasons, and what he desires, wills and believes, always depend on the man he is, and nothing connected with him can be presumed to be irrelevant to the conclusions he arrives at. (88:107, 108)

94. Bergson on the difference between the intellect and the will regarding the issue of simplicity:

> What is simple for our understanding is not necessarily so for our will. In cases where logic affirms that a certain road should be the shortest, experience intervenes, and finds that in that direction there is no road. (7:53; see also 7:97, 99)

95. Such a principle as *agape* cannot develop even intellectually without a strong volitional foundation; even though it involves a formal principle, above all other principles, it cannot be volitionally abstract.

96. Marcel deals well with the difference between love and abstraction:

> Between love and intelligence, there can be no real divorce. Such a divorce is apparently consummated only when intelli-

gence is degraded—becomes merely cerebral; and, of course, when love reduces itself to mere carnal appetite. But this we must assert, and as forcibly as possible: where love on one side, where intelligence on the other, reach their highest expression, they cannot fail to meet: do not let us speak of their becoming identical, for there can be no mutual identity except between abstractions; intelligence and love are the most concrete things in the world, and at a certain level every great thinker has recognized this or had a presentment of it. (64:7)

97. Bergson on the distinction between closed (static) and dynamic (open) morality:

We have made the distinction between the closed and the open: would anyone place Socrates among the closed souls? There was irony running through Socratic teaching, and outbursts of lyricism were probably rare; but in the measure in which these outbursts cleared the road for a new spirit, they have been decisive for the future of humanity. (7:63)

98. Moral philosophy involves the wise use of ethical theory so that mankind may be raised to the highest possible state in this world. The concept 'highest' implies a scale of values with God's character at the top, and one's conception of the majesty and profundity of His character will depend upon the maturity of one's own spiritual experience. Nevertheless, regardless of one's level of experience, he must conceive of God's character in terms that do not violate the highest conceivable moral norms.

99. Even though value plays a prominent and necessary part in my outlook, it plays an ultimate part because God values me. I cannot value Him honestly unless I assume this first. My felt-value is not the main issue. Faith can go beyond felt-value and for this reason it can create value. But moral norms must judge my felt-values before I use them as a *dynamic*. (Compare 7:78.)

100. Bergson on putting moral theories into practice:

On the other hand, it is of religious dogmas and the metaphysical theories they imply that we generally think as soon as the word religion is mentioned; so that when religion is said to be the foundation of morality, we picture to ourselves a group of conceptions relating to God and the world, the acceptance of which is supposed to result in the doing of good. But it is quite clear that these conceptions, taken as such, influence our will and our conduct in the same way as theories may do, that is to say, ideas; we are here on the intellectual plane, and, as I hinted above, neither obligation nor the force which extends it can possibly originate in bare ideas, bare ideas affecting our will only to the extent which it pleases us to accept them or put them into practice. (7:98, 99)

101. Belief is a necessity for dynamic morality, belief in one's responsibility. Responsibility generates more *dynamic* than the abstraction of "pure freedom" because it liberates one from egoism and establishes freedom on an empirical level by surpassing it as a mere conceptual abstraction.

102. Human morality must proceed from motives which in turn must be tested by moral principles and their derived rules of conduct. The test of a moral motive is not the same thing as the power or creativity of the particular motive. It is the motive which constitutes human morality. The testing facilities are essentially made up of a moral theory and its derivatives and serve in a quasi-negative role due to its abstraction.

103. Hocking says on the simplicity of Christianity,

> It is of the essence of Christianity that its central teachings are simple.
>
> It was one aspect of the genius of Jesus that amid a rich store of earlier codes and doctrines he discerned what was essential and brought it to brief and forcible expression. The essence of the law he states in the two great commandments; the essence of right conduct in the Golden Rule; the essence of prayer in the Lord's Prayer; the essence of theology in the picture of God as Father; the essence of the social ideal in the vision of the Kingdom of Heaven among men.
>
> Christianity is not an easy teaching; but the qualifications for grasping it, the ear to hear and the will to obey, are primarily moral and were first achieved by untutored fishermen; whereas its difficulties are said to be chiefly for those who, ruled by their possessions or entangled in affairs or befogged by seeming wisdom, find it hard to return to the direct intuitions of childhood . . .
>
> And further, only a religion whose first principles are capable of the simplest formulation can become a religion for

the modern man, whether in the Orient or elsewhere. The religion which assumes too much knowledge of the supernatural realm, its system of heavens and hells, or its inner mechanisms of eternal justice, can no longer be a living issue. (29: 278, 279)

It may be added that this simplicity has been also a necessary key to the moral success of Christianity, which makes no clear separation between the moral and the spiritual.

104. Paton on the inadequacy of mere self-love:

Morality was not invented yesterday. Like science itself, it has a long history behind it. In the face of modern skepticism I propose to assume that—at least in extreme cases—we are able to distinguish between a good man and a bad, and between right and wrong actions. Such an assumption is not affected by the fact that good men are sometimes confused in their moral thinking and may allow self-interest to mislead them both in their judgments and in their conduct. This is merely a danger against which we have all to be on our guard.

On this assumption it is simply untrue to say, whether directly or indirectly, that a good man is one who is good at satisfying his impulses or at furthering his own happiness. Skill in attaining our ends and prudence or enlightened self-love have their own value, and even their own place in a morally good life; but in themselves they are self-centered and so far are directly opposed to morality. (79:292, 293)

105. H. D. Lewis makes a very strong point for the recognition of the concepts of guilt and responsibility. He suggests that a proper treatment of these notions would require drastic changes both in our contemporary ethical thought and practice. He says:

Moral philosophers do not seem to have had a great deal to say about guilt, and it would be easy to compile an impressive list of ethical treatises in which the subject is not mentioned at all. In recent ethics especially it has suffered much neglect. In theology, on the other hand, the problem of guilt has always remained to the fore, and of late it has also elicited the very lively interest of the psychologist. It is the moralist who remains aloof.

This is as regrettable as it is strange. For however important the problem of guilt may be, in some of its bearings, for religious thought or psychology, it is first and foremost an ethical problem. And when the moralists are reluctant to tackle some ethical question, and are content to hand it over to other disciplines, such as theology or psychology, which have an interest in it, the properly ethical features of that question are apt to be either overlaid altogether by extraneous considerations or distorted in some quasi-ethical religious or psychological form. Of this the treatment of the problem of guilt is an excellent example. (56:148; compare 56:94, 95, 145, 149, 153)

106. A. C. Garnett gives a good account of the polar nature of the moral life by showing that both extremes are real, but that virtue is prior:

In these days in which the machine has so greatly magnified all man's activities, that sinfulness has attained such colossal proportions in its collective manifestations that it has rightly received new emphasis in every philosophy of human nature and theory of the social order. But there is no good reason why a theism which has accepted the evolutionary interpretation of nature should be more impressed with man's sin and decadence than with his virtue and progress. Both are facts of life and history, and it is only the latter that makes the former possible. Without virtue there could be no knowledge of sin, and without progress there could be no decadence. (23:5)

107. C. I. Lewis on the necessity of moral decision in man:

Within his own life, he is unable to live from moment to moment, responding to the here and now as the felt poignancies of it move him to do. He both can and must live in the light of the future he anticipates and with the salt and savor of his remembered past. In action, he has a range of choice unknown to any other creature, vouchsafed to him by his capacity to forecast, in measure, the future as it will be and the possible as it can be, dependent on what he may decide to bring about. By the scope of his imaginative understanding, alternative futurities are spread out before him, each needing but the touch of his decisive act to become reality. That which he chooses will be actual by his deed, and the others will be forever left in the limbo of what might have been. But by the same token the freedom of irresponsibility is lost to him. He is open to remorse for what he has brought about or

184

what he failed to do: he cannot respond as present feeling incites him merely but must face the future with concern and act with care. What he chooses to bring about, he must thereafter recognize as his doing which he never can disown. His freedom of choice is the necessity of decision and the responsibility for what is chosen and decided. This freedom and this responsibility, whether as privilege or as burden, are a part of his inheritance as human; and the acceptance and exercise of them are the vocation of man. (54:15, 16)

108. C. I. Lewis on intelligence:

The first of these two abilities mentioned—cognitive apprehension of the future, the absent, and the possible, including cognitive appraisal of what is so envisaged as desirable or undesirable—is intelligence. And the second—the capacity to arrive at general convictions, deliberately adopted attitudes, and precepts of conduct, and to guide action by what they sanction—is rationality or reasonableness.

It is doubtful that what is connoted by these two words, "intelligence" and "rationality," represent distinct features of the human mentality. At least they hardly could exist apart. (54:86, 87)

109. In N. S. Khrushchev's "Secret" Speech, we see his disdain for egoism in the form of individualism:

Comrades! We must abolish the cult of the individual decisively, once and for all; we must draw the proper conclusions concerning both ideological-theoretical and practical work.

It is necessary for this purpose:

First, in a Bolshevik manner to condemn and to eradicate the cult of the individual as alien to Marxism-Leninism and not consonant with the principles of party leadership and the norms of party life and to fight inexorably all attempts at bringing back this practice in one form or another.

To return to and actually practice in all our ideological work the most important theses of Marxist-Leninist science about the people as the creator of history and as the creator of all the material and spiritual good of humanity, about the decisive role of the Marxist part in the revolutionary fight for the transformation of society, about the victory of Communism. (36:129)

110. Theologians also do not usually deal with the nature of belief, but essentially with the content of their own beliefs. Theology is trying too hard to bend belief into an argumentative tool and thereby misses the creative nature of belief on the moral level.

111. Rudolph Otto's book *The Idea of the Holy* has been the most perceptive effort to date on this concept of the holy. It has done much to disentangle the muddle around creative moral belief.

112. Bergson says,

> Humanity had to wait till Christianity for the idea of universal brotherhood, with its implication of equality of rights and the sanctity of the person, to become operative. (7:78)

LIST OF WORKS CITED

1   Aiken, H. D. *The Age of Ideology.* Boston: Houghton Mifflin Co., 1957.
2   Aristotle. *The Works of Aristotle.* 8 vols. Edited by W. D. Ross. Oxford: Oxford University Press, 1928.
3   Ayer, Alfred J. *Language, Truth and Logic.* London: V. Gollancz, Ltd., 1936.
4   Beck, L. J. *The Method of Descartes.* Oxford: Clarendon Press, 1952.
5   Berdyaev, Nicolas. *The Origin of Russian Communism.* Ann Arbor: University of Michigan Press, 1960.
6   Bergson, Henri. "Moral Values and Other Subjects," *The Personalist,* XLII (Spring, 1961).
7   Bergson, Henri. *The Two Sources of Morality and Religion.* New York: Doubleday & Company, Inc., 1935.
8   *Bible. The Revised Standard Version of the New Testament.* New York: Thomas Nelson & Sons, 1953.
9   Blakeley, Thomas J. *Soviet Scholasticism.* Dordrecht: D. Reidel Publishing Co., 1961.
10 Braithwaite, R. B. "Belief and Action," *Proceedings of the Aristotelian Society Supplement,* XX (July, 1946).
11 Buchman, Frank N. D. *Remaking the World.* London: Blandford Press, 1961.
12 Burns, Emile (ed.) *A Handbook of Marxism.* New York: International Publishers, 1935.
13 Cahn, Edmond. *The Predicament of Democratic Man.* New York: Macmillan Co., 1961.
14 Campbell, P. and Howard, P. *Remaking Men.* New York: Arrowhead Books, Inc., 1954.
15 Clough, Shepard B. *Basic Values of Western Civilization.* New York: Columbia University Press, 1960.
16 Condillac. *Treatise on the Sensations.* Translated by G. Carr. Los Angeles: University of Southern California, 1930.
17 Copleston, Frederick. *A History of Philosophy.* Vol. I, Westminster, Maryland: The Newman Press, 1946.
18 Copleston, Frederick. *A History of Philosophy.* Vol. IV, Westminster, Maryland: The Newman Press, 1953.
19 Descartes. *Philosophical Works.* Vol. I. Translated by E. S. Haldane and G. R. T. Ross. Cambridge: Cambridge University Press, 1912.

20 Descartes. *Philosophical Works.* Vol. II. Translated by E. S. Haldane and G. R. T. Ross. Cambridge: Cambridge University Press, 1912.

21 Dewey, John. *The Quest for Certainty.* New York: Minton, Balch & Co., 1929.

22 Feigl, H. "Logical Empiricism," *Readings in Philosophical Analysis.* Edited by H. Feigl and W. Sellars. New York: Appleton-Century-Crofts, 1949.

23 Garnett, A. C. *The Moral Nature of Man.* New York: The Ronald Press Co., 1952.

24 Garnett, A. C. "Relativism and Absolutism in Ethics," *Ethics,* LIV (July, 1944).

25 Gillispie, Charles C. *The Edge of Objectivity.* Princeton: Printon University Press, 1960.

26 Hepburn, R. W. "Vision and Choice in Morality," *Proceedings of the Aristotelian Society Supplement,* XXX (July, 1956).

27 Hill, T. E. *Contemporary Ethical Theories.* New York: Macmillan Co., 1950.

28 Hocking, William E. *The Coming World Civilization.* New York: Harper & Brothers, 1956.

29 Hocking, William E. *Living Religions and a World Faith.* London: George Allen & Unwin, Ltd., 1940.

30 Hocking, William E. *Man and the State.* New Haven: Yale University Press, 1926.

31 Hocking, William E. "Marcel and the Ground Issues of Metaphysics," *Journal of Philosophy and Phenomenological Research,* XIV (June, 1954).

32 Hocking, William E. *Types of Philosophy.* New York: Charles Scribner's Sons, 1959.

33 Hofstadter, Albert. "The Seriousness of Moral Philosophy," *Ethics,* LXVI (July, 1956).

34 Hume, David. *An Enquiry Concerning Human Understanding.* Chicago: The Open Court Publishing Co., 1904.

35 Hume, David. *A Treatise of Human Nature.* Chicago: The Open Court Publishing Co., 1927.

36 Jacobs, Dan N. (ed.) *The New Communist Manifesto and Related Documents.* Evanston, Illinois: Row, Peterson and Co., 1961.

37 Jenkins, Iredell. "The Significance of Conscience," *Ethics,* LXV (July, 1955).

38 Jowett, B. (trans.) *The Dialogues of Plato.* New York: Random House, 1937.

39 Kant, I. *Critique of Practical Reason: and Other Writings in*

Moral Philosophy. Translated and edited by L. W. Beck. Chicago: University of Chicago Press, 1950.

40 Kant, I. *Critique of Pure Reason*. New York: The Humanities Press, 1950.

41 Kant, I. *The Metaphysic of Ethics*. Edinburgh: Thomas Clark, 1836.

42 Kant, I. *Prolegomena to Any Future Metaphysic*. Translated by J. P. Mahaffy and J. H. Bernard. London: Macmillan Co., 1889.

43 Kaufman, Gordon D. *Relativism, Knowledge and Faith*. Chicago: University of Chicago Press, 1960.

44 Kierkegaard, S. *Purity of Heart Is to Will One Thing*. Translated by Douglas V. Steere. New York: Harper, 1938.

45 Kline, George L. "Soviet Morality, Current," *Encyclopedia of Morals*, Edited by V. Ferm. New York: Philosophical Library, 1956.

46 Laird, John. *Knowledge, Belief and Opinion*. New York: Century Co., 1930.

47 Laird, John. *A Study of Moral Theory*. London: George Allen and Unwin, 1926.

48 Lamprecht, Sterling P. "Empiricism and Natural Knowledge," *University of California Publications in Philosophy*. Vol. XVI. Berkeley: University of California Press, 1940.

49 Lenin, V. I. *Marx Engels Marxism*. Moscow: Foreign Languages Publishing House, 1951.

50 Lerner, Max. *Ideas Are Weapons*. New York: Viking Press, 1939.

51 Lewis, C. I. *An Analysis of Knowledge and Valuation*. La Salle: The Open Court Publishing Co., 1946.

52 Lewis, C. I. *The Ground and Nature of the Right*. New York: Columbia University Press, 1955.

53 Lewis, C. I. *Mind and the World-Order*. New York: Dover Publications Inc., 1956.

54 Lewis, C. I. *Our Social Inheritance*. Bloomington: Indiana University Press, 1957.

55 Lewis, H. D. (ed.) *Contemporary British Philosophy*. London: Allen & Unwin, 1956.

56 Lewis, H. D. *Morals and Revelation*. London: Allen & Unwin, 1951.

57 Locke, John. *An Essay Concerning Human Understanding*. 2 vols. Oxford: Clarendon Press, 1894.

58 Locke, John. *Essays on the Law of Nature*. Edited by W. von Leyden. Oxford: Clarendon Press, 1954.

59 Locke, John. *Two Treatises of Government*. Edited by Peter Laslett. Cambridge: Cambridge University Press, 1960.

60 Lovejoy, A. O. *Reflections on Human Nature*. Baltimore: Johns Hopkins Press, 1961.

61 MacIver, R. M. *The Web of Government*. New York: Macmillan Co., 1947.

62 Mannheim, Karl. *Ideology and Utopia*. New York: Harcourt Brace, 1936.

63 Marcel, G. (ed.) *Fresh Hope for the World*. London: Longmans, 1960.

64 Marcel, G. *Man Against Mass Society*. Chicago: Regnery, 1952.

65 Marx, Karl. *Capital*. New York: Dutton & Co., 1934.

66 Marx, Karl and Engels, Friedrich. *The German Ideology*. New York: International Publishers, 1939.

67 Miller, K. Bruce. *The Dynamic of the Numinous Consciousness in Altruism*. Master's Thesis. Baylor University, 1952.

68 Moore, G. E. *Principia Ethica*. Cambridge: Cambridge University Press, 1903.

69 Moral Re-Armament. *Ideology and Co-Existence*. Mackinac Island, 1959.

70 Mowat, R. C. *Climax of History*. London: Blandford Press, 1951.

71 Mure, G. R. G. *Retreat From Truth*. Oxford: Blackwell, 1958.

72 Naess, Arne. *Democracy, Ideology and Objectivity*. Oslo: Oslo University Press, 1956.

73 Northrop, F. S. C. *Ideological Differences and World Order*. New Haven: Yale University Press, 1949.

74 Northrop, F. S. C. *The Meeting of East and West*. New York: Macmillan Co., 1960.

75 Northrop, F. S. C. *The Taming of the Nations*. New York: Macmillan Co., 1953.

76 Northrop, F. S. C. *Understanding the Contemporary World*. Occasional Paper No. 50. Honolulu: University of Hawaii, July, 1949, no page numbers in publication.

77 Nygren, Anders. *Agape and Eros*. Translated by Philip S. Watson. Philadelphia: The Westminster Press, 1953.

78 Otto, Rudolph. *The Idea of the Holy*. London: Oxford University Press, 1950.

79 Paton, H. J. *The Modern Predicament*. London: George Allen & Unwin, 1955.

80 Polanyi, Michael. *Personal Knowledge*. Chicago: University of Chicago Press, 1958.

81 Price, H. H. "Clarity Is Not Enough," *Proceedings of the Aristotelian Society Supplement*, XIX (July, 1945).

82 Price, H. H. *Perception*. London: Methuen, 1950.

83 Prichard, Harold A. *Moral Obligation*. Oxford: Clarendon Press, 1949.

84 Ravines, Eudocio. *The Yenan Way*. New York: Scribner, 1951.

85 Ross, W. D. *Foundations of Ethics*. Oxford: Clarendon Press, 1939.

86 Rothstein, A. (ed.) *History of the Communist Party of the Soviet Union* (abbreviated as *History of the C.P.S.U.*). Moscow: Foreign Languages Publishing House, 1960.

87 Roucek, Joseph S. "A History of the Concept of Ideology," *Journal of the History of Ideas*, IV (October, 1944).

88 Schiller, F. *Problems of Belief*. London: Hodder & Stoughton, 1924.

89 Schoeck, H. and Wiggins, J. (ed.) *Scientism and Values*. Princeton: Van Nostrand, 1960.

90 Smith, N. K. *New Studies in the Philosophy of Descartes*. London: Macmillan Co., 1952.

91 Stalin, Joseph. *Leninism*. Vol. II. New York: International Publishers, no date.

92 Tsanoff, Radoslav. "Moral Principles and National Interests," *Ethics*, LXII (July, 1952).

93 Webb, Sidney and Beatrice. *Soviet Communism*. 2 vols. New York: Scribner's, 1936.

94 Werkmeister, W. H. *Theories of Ethics*. Lincoln, Nebraska: Johnsen Publishing Co., 1961.

95 Whitehead, A. N. *Science and the Modern World*. New York: Macmillan Co., 1926.

96 Wood, Ledger. *The Analysis of Knowledge*. London: George Allen & Unwin, 1940.

97 Xenophon. *Works*. Vol. III, Part I. Translated by H. G. Dakyns. London: Macmillan, 1897.

98 Yates, B. Lund. "Dr. Frank N. D. Buchman's Contribution to Contemporary Religious Thought," *The Hibbert Journal*, LVII (October, 1958).

99 Zeller, Eduard. *Outlines of the History of Greek Philosophy*. London: Kegan Paul, Trench, Trubner & Co., 1931.

100 "Ethics, History of," *Encyclopedia Britannica*. Vol. VIII. 1958.

101 *New English Dictionary*. Vol. V, Pt. 2. Oxford: Clarendon Press, 1928.

102 "The Ideology That Wins—A Challenge to Communism," U. S. *Congressional Record*. 86th Cong., 2d Sess., 1960.

103 *Los Angeles Herald-Examiner*. May 6, 1963, p. A21.

191

INDEX

193

INDEX

194

INDEX

195

INDEX

INDEX

197

INDEX

INDEX